REAL MEN

Don't Abandon Their Responsibilities

by Dr. Harold Voth

HUNTINGTON HOUSE PUBLISHERS

Huntington House Publishers
P.O. Box 53788
Lafayette, Louisiana 70505

Library of Congress Card Catalog Number 93-77298
ISBN 1-56384-038-3

Contents

Preface

It is usually taken for granted that stalwart Americans will always exist and that America will forever extend a protective wing over less powerful nations. But no generation is ever like the preceding one. New life replaces the old every moment. What are the new arrivals like? What values do they live by? Will they advance our way of life to new levels of excellence or will they adopt ways of life that lead to disintegration?

The basic fabric of our society is changing, and as it changes so do our people change. The trend is toward disintegration; a devitalizing process is at work, involving individual and social factors in a vicious and downhill cycle. A nation low in vitality and national will always loses out in one way or another to more vigorous nations. The interaction of personal and social factors is so firm that at present the future is by no means certain or clear. One can only hope that there will be enough people of strength, vision, and the capacity to take responsibility to intervene decisively before it is too late. The crucial question is whether or not the present trend in America is reversible.

The vitality of a nation is a reflection of the aggregate vitality of its people. In America we have been fortunate to have had the great energy of our people channeled by laws and customs that have permitted individuality to be expressed in such a way as to lead to social vitality and to excellence. People had the freedom to grow, innovate, create, and master great social challenges. We became the most powerful, efficient, and generous nation of all time.

This book examines the American scene and explains why it is destroying itself and our children both literally and in spirit.

This is a tragic time in the history of our nation. Not too long ago parents could give their children a good start in life and be reasonably certain that the society into which they entered as children and young adults would not destroy them. This is no longer so. Even children from the most stable families are highly vulnerable to extremely destructive social forces. Illegitimate children, children from broken homes, and those from unstable families are virtually helpless with regard to the social revolution, which will destroy them. Because of their weakness of personality, they will be drawn into ways of living that not only destroy them, but they in turn will contribute to the destruction of our country by adopting these destructive ways of life.

In addition to social changes, which are contributing to the destruction of people, young ones in particular, the family, from which all life springs, is crumbling. Families are breaking up at an alarming rate.

The stable heterosexual commitment is rapidly becoming a thing of the past. The authority of the male has diminished and increasing numbers of men show a marked irresponsibility toward their families and are heads of their households in name only. Not only is the status of males being diminished, but many men are becoming feminine in their appearance, attitudes, and behavior, and many women are becoming masculine in the same ways. Increasing numbers of women are avoiding their responsibilities as wives and mothers and believe their future lies in pursuing those objectives that once were the province of the male. Social and economic factors are forcing mothers to work and children into day-care centers or into the hands of unconcerned, and often transient, caretakers. For these various reasons, children are being deprived of the most vital experience of all—good family life. The effects on children when their father is not a strong, masculine man and their mother a strong, feminine woman, when a strong family bond fails to exist, or when families disintegrate defies estimation. The cycle of sick or weak people who are the product of sick or broken families keeps repeating itself, the effects spread from one generation to the next, and slowly but surely the sickness tears down the best traditions of mankind, which made our society strong.

As a psychiatrist and psychoanalyst it has been my privilege for forty years to see a very personal, detailed and in-depth view of the human condition. It seems to me that there is a clear and definite link between the forces of sickness inside people and the current trends in society. A cyclical reinforcement exists between the individual and society. Sick people are "castrated" people, that is, forces within them prevent them from being competent and masterful men and women who can make a commitment to each other, create a family, and eventually replace themselves with healthy human beings. There is an alarming increase of such people in our land, a fact which, when seen in the context of the radical changes in norms and values, leads to my belief that ours is becoming a castrated land and therefore a land in great peril.

Our nation will ultimately suffer. A nation has to be cared for like anything else. That is done by preserving its best traditions, customs, and social patterns and by socializing each new generation to embrace these values and advance them to new and higher levels of excellence. Strong, healthy people make strong societies. A nation filled with sick, devitalized people will eventually decline. This book will explain some of the reasons America is destroying itself.

PART ONE

The Family:
The Source of Human Vitality

Chapter One

The Source of Human Vitality

It is an error to believe that America, the invincible, will always be. There is no Iron Law guaranteeing that generous and stalwart Americans will always exist. The American dream is not forever safe. These ideas are illusions, born of self-deception. An internal process is at work in our country which poses a far greater danger to us than dwindling natural resources, the energy crisis, our huge national debt, or the trade deficit.

While it is true that technological advances, abundance of natural resources—in short, environmental and sociological factors—have a great deal to do with how far a society advances, personal factors or forces within the individual, that is, the vitality of a people, really make the difference. Social values, traditions, our constitutions, and laws channel individual vitality in ways that cause a people to develop into a great society or divert it in other directions. In America we have had the resources, the technological developments, the way of life, *and the individual vitality* that have made this the greatest nation of all time.

The pattern of life in America is changing very dramatically. The divorce rate is approaching 50 percent with second marriages failing at a rate close to 60 per-

11

cent. Millions of young people are living together without taking the formal step of marriage. The illegitimacy
rate is approximately 20 percent. In large cities, the rate
is much higher: 50 percent in Washington, D.C.; 33 percent in New York City; and 30 percent in Chicago. In
Chicago alone that means two hundred thousand babies
are born each year without a set of parents to rear them.

One-third of American children do not have their
fathers in their home. Only 60 percent of American children today live with both biological parents.[1] By age
eighteen, one-half of American children will be living
apart from their fathers. The poverty rate of children
living only with their mother is at 55 percent, five times
the rate for children living with two parents.[2]

The simple truth is that the heterosexual bond—the
capacity for a man and a woman to remain lovingly
committed to each other—has become very fragile. This
is an exceedingly ominous sign, for it is upon this bond
that the fate of any society depends.

In addition to outright broken homes and situations
that never were families, increasing numbers of marriages are severely strained because of personality disturbances of the couple and social pressures. These
strains and disturbances also have a profound effect on
the developing child and eventually lead to personality
disturbances of many different kinds in him.

Finally, the mass exodus of women from the home is
having a damaging effect on young children. The work
force is now one-half women. Forty-five percent of these
women have preschool children, and 50 percent or more
have children of ages ranging up to adolescence. The
absent mother has a disastrous effect on the development of the young, especially when the continuity of the
mother-child relationship is broken during the first three
years of life.[3]

It has been estimated that if these trends continue,
within a few years nearly one-half of our young adults
will have grown up in some arrangement other than the
classical family for some portion of their development,

that is, in a home where father was breadwinner and mother the homemaker caring for two or three children. One study reported that today only 20 percent of our families are of this classical configuration. This is the kind of family that produced the solid people that made America the strongest nation of all time.

Emotionally sick parents or broken homes or part-time homes do not turn out high percentages of emotionally healthy boys and girls. Children from such homes grow up to be emotionally disturbed adults. Because of what is happening to the American family, the number of emotionally disturbed people is increasing geometrically, that is, in ever-expanding numbers. Sick individuals eventually create a sick and weak society by changing the structure of their society and by weakening the national will. It is just that simple. I know of no possible way for America to retain its vitality, its preeminence among nations, with this trend in process. The family has produced people with the backbone, the spirit, the creativity, the productivity, and the strength to have made this nation what it became. Family life in America is crumbling like a sand castle in the way of a great wave of self-destruction.

Men, women, boys, and girls must have a certain amount of vitality and freedom from crippling emotional illness to be able to get through life and not experience a sense of defeat when faced with life's challenges. There is nothing mysterious about emotional health and individual vitality, and we know very well what produces emotional illnesses that cripple and, at times, destroy people. I have worked as a psychiatrist for thirty years, and as a psychoanalyst for twenty, and the evidence that I have seen, as have many of my colleagues, is overwhelming as regard to what is required for babies and children to become healthy, mature men and women who can take hold of life, do something constructive with it, and embrace values, traditions, and institutions that advance the society. These strong people avoid those ways of life that destroy them as well as society itself.

The crucible from which all life springs is the family. The events within the family can make or break the individual, and collectively, the civilization. This fundamental unit is the building block, and has been the building block of all social organizations from the tribe, village, and on to the most highly developed societies and civilizations. Will Durant said the family can survive without the state, but without the family all is lost. Therefore, not only must the family survive, but its internal workings must function in ways that turn out strong men and women—not weak ones who eventually become casualties of one form or another or who may work actively against the best values and traditions of our country.

A newborn child contains great potential, but in order for that potential to be unlocked, evoked, developed, and expressed, certain fundamental events must take place early in its life. When these events occur imperfectly or do not occur at all, the developing child will become a social liability in one form or another rather than an asset, or if he becomes an asset, he may never achieve his full potential.

The underpinnings of personality are biologic underpinnings. None are more fundamental than the biologic imperatives that lead to the psychologic qualities of maleness and femaleness. There are, of course, an array of other potentialities. One of the most fundamental functions of parenting is to evoke, develop, and reinforce gender identity and then proceed to shepherd the developing child in such a way as to bring his psychological side into harmony with his biological side, and thereby develop a solid sense of maleness or femaleness.

Sexual identity is intimately woven into the overall fabric of personality. Human beings are not biologically bisexual, despite what the gay liberationists and some feminists would have us believe. The human spirit is greatly impaired when childhood development does not lead to fully developed masculinity or femininity. Fully masculine men and feminine women are by definition mature, and that term implies the ability to live out one's abilities. These include the capacity to mate, live in harmony with a member of the opposite sex, and carry out the responsibilities of parenthood. Mature people are competent and masterful; not only can they make families but they can take hold of life generally and advance it, and in particular they can replace themselves with healthy children who become healthy men and women. Mature individuals can, of course, elect to not have children and deploy all of their energies into their work. However, the fate of individual human development and of mankind depends on the durability of the heterosexual relationship, and the stability and integrity of the family.

–   The correct development of a child requires the commitment of mature parents who understand either consciously or intuitively that children do not grow up like Topsy. Good mothering from birth onward provides the psychological core upon which all subsequent development takes place. *Mothering is probably the most important human function on earth*. This is a full-time, demanding task. It requires a high order of gentleness, commitment, steadiness, capacity to give, and many other qualities, too. A woman needs a good man by her side so she will not be distracted and depleted by too many other responsibilities. With his help, she will be able to provide rich humanness to her babies and children. Her needs must be met by the man. Above all, she must be made secure. A good man brings out the best in a woman, who can then do her best for the children. Similarly, a good woman brings out the best in a man, who can then do his best for his wife and children. Children bring out the best in their parents. All together they make a family, a place where people of great strength are shaped, who in turn make strong societies. Our nation was built by such people.

Strength of personality, individual vitality, competence, the capacity for mastery, the factors that make up a complete being, are not so mysterious. We know what kinds of experiences the developing child requires in

order for him to develop these characteristics. These
experiences are provided in the context of the classical
family. At earlier times in our history, social forces more
readily permitted the expression of certain Laws of Nature which led to the formation of this classical family.

The heterosexual bond reflects the workings of one
of Nature's most fundamental laws. The animal king-
dom depends on it. Male and female are different and
these qualities have biological underpinnings; that is,
there are biologic laws that account for the difference
between the sexes.[4] These differences attract each other,
and because of this attraction, it is possible for the family to form as the young are born. There are laws that
govern childhood development. When these are violated,
a great variety of personality disturbances result.

Even though the complexities of social life have vastly
increased, this basic model of the family is as valid today and as consistent with the natural endowments of
male and female as it was in primitive times. The family
may reside on Park Avenue or on an isolated farm or in
the jungle, but the basic qualitative differences between
male and female remain the same. The integrity of the
family, the care and proper psychological development
of the young depend on the appropriate expression or
living out of these differences. When environmental factors prevent the man and woman who make a family
from living out the qualities with which Nature endowed
them and from maintaining a family unit, serious consequences follow.

To say that the man is the final authority in no way
implies that he should be a tyrant, a dictator, a marti-
net, or have his way in all matters. What is best for the
entire family should be the principle that guides the
decision-making process within the family. The discovery of what is best may require much discussion among
the family members. Someone must, however, have the
final word.

The father should be loving, compassionate, understanding, capable of gentleness and the like—but all
should know he is the protector, the one who is ulti-

mately responsible for the integrity and survival of the family. It is known that the most successful families are those where all members, including the wife, look up to the father-husband.

Controlling and channeling the instincts and impulses of infants and children and developing their potentialities to the fullest extent, imparting the best in human values to them, require the best efforts of both the man and the woman. However, clear divisions of responsibility and labor must exist; some special responsibilities and authority are the mother's; other special responsibilities and authority are the father's. There must be no role confusion between the mother and father, and though these distributions of responsibility and authority exist, everyone in the family must also know, appreciate and respect the fact that the father has the overall responsibility for the family; he is its chief executive, but like all good executives he should listen to all within his organization.

No organization functions well with weak leadership—nor can the family. Strong and just leaders build strong organizations; this is equally true of the family. A really strong leader will evoke strength and bring out the best in everyone within his organization and at the same time maintain a functioning hierarchic structure. However, we are rapidly becoming a fatherless society; if the trend continues I believe society as we know it will collapse. Families cannot exist without fathers. Without families society cannot exist.

There are those who say that parental roles are learned, that men and women have been forced into these roles by social conventions. I do not believe this. If this were true, then the consequences of male and female role confusion or reversal and the failure of the man to be the head of the family would not be as serious, productive of illness, and tragic as they often are.

Far-reaching and serious consequences result when internal family arrangements deviate from the norm. Virtually every patient I have personally treated, or whose treatment I have supervised, or whose treatment

I have studied through a research endeavor, has revealed an aberrant family constellation. The most common pattern was the family in which the mother was domineering and aggressive and the father weak and passive. Some of these fathers were aggressive and assertive in their work situations but timid and weak in relation to their wives. The wives in these marriages clearly "wore the pants." Another pattern was that of a weak mother who tended to cling to her children, and a tyrannical father who was dictatorial but incapable of experiencing closeness to his wife or children. While it may seem that such a father is head of the family, actually much of the responsibility and authority falls to the wife except for periods when the father makes his presence felt by angry, usually irrational, outbursts. Some women are forced to fill the role of both mother and father by necessity. These women may be feminine but the absence of the father places all of the responsibilities on them; the effects of this family pattern on children as well as on these mothers are not good. Fathers and mothers may be hostile, rejecting, overly anxious, or possessive. Some families lack any semblance of an authority structure. Some parents live up to their responsibilities sporadically. All of these conditions within the family adversely affect the child's personality development.

Strong fathers and strong mothers (in the feminine sense—strong femininity is not aggressiveness), who love each other, who cooperate with each other, and whose roles are clearly defined, produce healthy children. When this pattern is disturbed in any of a number of ways, emotional disturbances of a wide variety are the result in the children. Two studies illustrate this point. One is by Reinhardt wherein he points out that outstanding naval pilots have a strong bond with their fathers.[5] The other is by Vaillant who reports the results of a twenty-nine-year study in which the family patterns of ninety-five men were described.[6] One of the most striking findings is that when these men perceived their mothers to be the dominant one in their family they were more often poorly adjusted or mentally ill. These are but two research studies; literally hundreds of clinical studies and reports which link mental illness to dominant mothers and weak fathers fill professional journals.

The results are diverse, and all can be subsumed under the heading of personality disturbances. Many of these disturbances are in harmony with some of the new "norms" of society. The origins of these disturbances inevitably pointed to parents who were ill themselves and to family patterns which fell short of the ideal.

Childhood experiences within the family, and their subsequent effects, have been implicated in all of the psychiatric illnesses (psychoses and neuroses), personality disorders, perversions, homosexuality, transsexuality, transvestism, drug addiction, alcoholism, delinquency, suicide, crime, the current blurring of sex roles (which is becoming widespread at an alarming rate), child abuse, divorce, and failure to adapt to life generally or in specific instances. Those persons afflicted in one or more of the preceding ways contribute to the weakening of our society, parts of which are very sick. Conversely, healthy parents produce healthy children. The aborigines of Australia have the oldest living culture despite the harsh environment in which they live. This is based on an indestructible family unit, the fundamental elements of which (father, mother, and offspring) are reinforced by relatives. There is no role confusion regarding male and female, nor homosexuality, in this culture.

The family is the unit within which the child develops courage, self-confidence, the ability to trust, autonomy, a sense of inner authority, and the capacity to be masterful. Here the biological qualities of male and female are evoked and reinforced by experiences with parents. The capacity to love blossoms; sexuality is awakened. Out of these experiences man and woman learn to form a loving, intimate, and cooperative relationship and to set up rules for their small organization (the family) wherein the best can be evoked in their children and in themselves as well. Learning to cooperate with others begins in the family; the process of socialization begins and is developed there. The male is, in a sense, the key in that he is ultimately responsible, and yet the woman is equally important, for without good mothering boys and girls do not develop into men and women who can make good families. The roles of father and mother and their responsibilities are different but both are essential.

Nothing of what has been said in any way demeans the woman or exalts the man. If a man and woman wish to form an organization—a family—then there must be rules of operation by which the members of that organization shall be guided. These rules must be harmonious with the biological qualities of the male and female and the social responsibilities of each. Once the children are out of the home, social roles of male and female can change and new responsibilities can be taken on, especially by the woman.

Having a family is one of the highest callings on earth; children are our most precious and valuable resource. Their care should fall only to those who are suitable for the task. Many people who are capable of living productive lives should remain unmarried. Others are capable of marriage but should never have children. Ideally, children should be born only to those who can fulfill this highest of all callings; these are men and women who are fully male and female and who are not burdened by personality disturbances and/or psychiatric illness, and who have the time to make the family a primary career. Such individuals will then be able to organize the family structure in such a way as to evoke and reinforce in their children the finest that Nature has to give.

But the home is not a place just for children; it is important for men and women too. Even after children are in school, having a secure home to which children and husband can return and escape from the stresses of life is vital. Only a healthy woman can provide such a setting and atmosphere. To be able to regularly return to this atmosphere where one is known and loved replenishes the spirit. The marvelous quality which exists within a happy home cannot be duplicated anywhere. A family is precious, and the surest way to preserve it is for men and women to fully understand that one of the highest responsibilities to humanity is the making of a home and family.

Research studies and countless clinical reports provide scientific and clinical validation for what every student of the Bible knows. The Bible spells out these same principles for the organization of the family. In other words, the classical family works best and turns out the healthiest children. In my entire career I have never had a woman patient, no matter how militant a feminist or disturbed, fail to spontaneously divulge her secret wish for a strong man in her life—father when she was a child and husband as an adult woman, even though on the surface she may claim the opposite.

A woman who can live in harmony with a strong man will herself be a strong woman. These two will not clash or compete with each other. Rather they will divide up responsibilities, and live and work in harmony. I did not create or manufacture these patterns; I am merely reporting them. It is simply a fact that a family with a weak man suffers and children do not turn out as well.

When the personalities of parents are crippled by psychological conflicts, in particular those which impair a clear sense of maleness or femaleness, or when children are deprived of the continuous commitment of mothers and fathers (the mother in particular) during the first few years of life, developmental disturbances occur in children of varying degrees of severity, depending on the time and duration of parental absence or the degree of severity of the personality disturbances in the parents. The developmental disturbances in the children may show up in childhood, or they may go underground only to surface years later when life begins to make its demands on them, especially when they attempt to make families of their own.

The most serious crisis facing us today is that of the family, the alterations of its internal structure, the high incidence of its dissolution, and the associated crisis of the human spirit. The fate of the family is in the hands of the man and woman who form it, and in the hands of the society which supplies its support. The family is in danger because the personalities of men and women are increasingly less mature, the distinction between male and female is less clear, and because social values which maintain or support sex role differences and the family are changing.

I believe all responsible people should oppose the blurring of values which distinguish male from female. I decry those social groups which advocate unisex life-styles and which impose their values on young children in schools and nurseries through their efforts to obscure the differences between male and female. While freedom of the printed word is essential to a free society, it is unfortunate that so much favorably tilted publicity is given to those who have failed in their roles as adults and parents and who advocate, for instance, homosexual marriages as a suitable way to rear children, or who abdicate their responsibilities to home and young children and would have the husband care for children while the wife is working outside the home. Such nonsense is being taught in universities.

The consequences of open marriage, communal living, mate swapping, or living together and having children without serious commitment between the man and woman have never been tested, and yet these ways of living are being openly advocated. The consequences of the half-hearted heterosexual commitments many people make might not be so serious if children were never born out of such arrangements, but they are, and these children are deprived of mature parents and good family life. When society openly endorses such life-styles, the door is opened wider for emotionally disturbed young people to follow these life-styles. Like it or not, these people have children. Who will care for them?

Society should do all it can to reverse the present trends. It should emphasize the differences between the sexes and make it possible for boys and men to be as masculine as possible and for children to become adults who can form strong heterosexual relationships, marry, and produce normal children. These changes would be preventive psychiatry at its best. What psychiatry does now as prevention is pitifully inadequate.

If all goes well, the effects of family life can evoke the best that Nature has to give; if not, family life can have disastrous consequences. Since the family provides the foundation for personality and for civilization, it is imperative that its structure and functioning be so arranged as to bring out the best in children. Children become the adults society and civilization depend on. It is essential that the effects of family life be clearly understood by those who produce children. The solution lies in salvaging the family and the way of family life which produces healthy children.

Doing anything in life halfway is not as good as doing it well. The relevance of this principle is nowhere greater than for the family. Our goal should be to reserve the high responsibility and privilege of rearing children to those who are themselves most mature, and this means masculine males and feminine females.

Those pioneers who developed America possessed great inner strength. They came from strong families. There was no ambiguity about male or female. Their will prevailed because they had received generously from their mothers and fathers. Fathers were men of strength, direction, and authority. Family ties were close and solid. America became the greatest, strongest, and most generous nation of all time. Her greatness today depends even more upon the strength and vitality of the family and its impact upon the individual and society.

Chapter Two

Childhood and the Impact of Parenting

Personality development is the result of the interaction of environmental factors and constitutional (hereditary) factors. Guided by the principles of human development, the rewards to the child, to the parents, and to society are enormous.

Constitutional Factors

Just as there are genetically determined differences in physical characteristics—body build, color of eyes and hair, etc.—so, too, are there wide variations in psychological and behavioral characteristics which are inborn. At birth some infants are placid and quiet, while others are restless and active. These qualities are traceable, or so it seems, into adulthood. Some persons are quiet by nature, tend to desire solitude; as they grow older they tend to restrict their social contacts. Others are just the opposite; they enjoy socialization, and need more contact with the external environment. These differences are normal. Some people show mixtures of both kinds of these opposite tendencies. It is an unsettled question as to what extent and which traits of personality have their origin in constitution and to what extent these traits are acquired through life experience. In some persons talents and skills seem to be inborn. "Basic" intelligence is constitutionally determined but its successful application is largely due to environmental influences.

It is crucial for the happy outcome of the child's early development that parents and other adults (teachers, relatives, etc.) recognize the constitutional uniqueness of the child (particularly those qualities which are typically male or female) and not force him to become the kind of person which is contrary to his basic nature. An aspect of the art of parenthood is to be able to recognize these qualities of a child's personality and adapt to them in a way that leads to a harmonious interaction between parent and child.

Certain basic qualities of personality fit with certain vocations, professions, and avocations in later life. Parents should provide the kind of exposures to situations so that the child can eventually discover where he fits best and where his native potentialities can best be evoked and developed.

The most fundamental constitutional factor of all has to do with the qualities of maleness and femaleness. Much has been written about gender, and various theories have been proposed. Some believe they have strong evidence for a biologic force, male as distinct from female, which shines through despite a host of unnatural, gender-confusing, environmental influences. I believe this is correct. That gender identity is also determined by environmental factors (this refers mainly to the parental attitudes toward the child very early in life) is unmistakably clear. A careful review of the concepts of what factors influence gender identity leads me to conclude that man is not biologically bisexual—that he is not both male and female. It appears that the embryo is bipotential very early but that certain hormonal events occur within the embryo which cause it to develop into male or female and not a mixture of both. These hormonal effects not only determine the obvious sexual anatomical differences but bring about brain changes and behavioral differences in boys and girls.

Of all the traits which deserve the clearest understanding and the respect of parents and society at large, the traits of maleness and femaleness are the most important. When parental influence, life-styles, roles, and social values which are not in harmony with basic maleness and femaleness are forced upon the child, great harm with far-reaching consequences to the child, and later to his children, results. The paternal and maternal instincts are a function of and expression of biologic maleness and femaleness.

It bears repeating that powerful forces within the family and society are complicating the development of children by forcing values and life-styles upon them which do not permit the fullest development and expression of maleness and femaleness. For example, some teachers in nursery and elementary schools are introducing play techniques which blur sex differences rather then distinguish them. Clothing styles make it difficult to tell a male from a female at a distance—and in some cases even up close. Hair styles reflect this blurring. The unisex movement and aspects of the women's liberation movement contribute to this blurring. The trend is to erase sex differences, not to accentuate them. These social trends run counter to natural law; Nature designed male and female as distinct and different. The environment, parents in particular, should evoke and reinforce these differences, not blur them or—worse—attempt to reverse them. When a child begins to manifest the qualities of the opposite sex, positive evidence is at hand that improper *psychological* development is taking place and *not* that his biologic nature is the basis for these changes. These qualities can be changed and this should be done as quickly as possible.

There are, of course, human qualities common to both sexes which have nothing to do with gender identity and their appearance in the child is no cause for alarm. Both sexes should be able to express a wide range of human qualities such as tenderness, gentleness, love, anger, compassion, sensitivity, creativeness, etc. It is

quite natural for a little boy to pick up certain traits or
mannerisms from his mother, and the little girl from her
father, and in no way be destined for a disturbance of
their identity. However, when this occurs excessively it
is likely that the child's identification process is not proceeding properly. The terms "boy" and "girl" have powerful meanings and should unequivocally be the guiding
principles for the child's upbringing once the sex of the
child has been established at birth. No little boy or girl
should ever be treated as if he were of the opposite sex.
There are, unfortunately, far too many parents who behave in such a way as to force their children to develop
in a direction which is contrary to nature. Men are just
as guilty as women, although the effects of women dis-
turb gender development more profoundly because their
effects on the child come much earlier in the child's life.

Environmental Factors

The environmental factors which influence childhood
development refer primarily to influences within the family. How a child is reared will, to a large extent, determine the final form his personality will take and how
successfully and effectively he lives his life, including
whether or not he will become mentally ill. It bears
repeating that those parents who are unmixed in their
sexual identity—that is, the father is fully masculine
and normal and the mother, similarly, is fully feminine
and normal—produce the healthiest children.

Normal parents are persons who remain free of symptoms within the context of a good marriage and who can
live out their sexual identity and skills and abilities in
appropriate social roles. Good parents love each other
and can experience full sexual pleasure with each other.
Neither will find it necessary or desirable to have lovers
or isolated sexual experiences with others. They will be
able to cooperate with each other; competitiveness will
be absent. Each will feel that his or her own gender is
equally valuable as the other. Each will respect the other
and neither will demean the opposite sex.

Mothers

A normal woman is one whose own development was such as to permit her to achieve a full flowering of her femininity. Such a woman cannot completely fulfill herself unless she marries and has children—at least one child—and, ideally, only such women should have children. To exclude men and children from her life would be a heavy burden. She would be forced to find substitute gratifications for her maternal urges and her natural tendency to experience loving and being loved by a man as well as sexual pleasure with him.

A normal woman will want to nurse her infant and unless there are extenuating circumstances which prevent her, or a physiologic insufficiency, she will and should do so. These early life experiences are critical in their importance, especially for the baby but also for the mother. A strong bond develops between the mother and infant through this experience. Nursing her baby, consistently responding to its needs, and the other features of infant care, are experiences which have a maturing effect on the mother.

Through the nursing experience and others with the mother, the infant receives the gentleness and nurture which form the core of personality. It is very important for a mother to hold her child, to rock it while nursing, and to rock it to sleep. A rocking chair is the most important piece of furniture in her home.

These good mothering experiences "fill" the child, and all through life this fortunate individual will silently experience the calm and gentle reassurance of his good mother inside of him. The foundations of personality will have been formed, and if subsequent developmental phases progress well the likelihood of mental illness for the child is nil and the chances of a full and rewarding life are great, assuming the existence of opportunities in society. Some of the finest adult characteristics can be attributed to good, bountiful, and loving mothering. These include an inner sense of goodness and strength, security, generosity, courage, trust, the capacity to love, an ability to form meaningful, intimate, cooperative, and enduring relationships with both sexes, and the ability to experience sexual pleasure in a mature form with the opposite sex. Success in work and play is dependent to a large degree on having had a good mother.

This mother will, above all, experience her child as a separate individual and not a possession from which she dreads to part. As the child begins to explore his environment, the mature and feminine mother will always give reassurance, never hold the child back but will always be there should the child become afraid and need to retreat to a more secure position. Such encouragement to venture into the environment, and the reassurance when fear and insecurity strike, provide the basis for the child's capacity for mastery during subsequent developmental periods, and on through all of life. By means of a series of separations and safe returns to his mother the child develops a sense of separateness and inner security without forming excessive separation anxiety, and the discovery will have been made that the environment can be mastered.

As a consequence of this good mothering the child does not have to cling constantly to his mother or a substitute. Such childhood experiences make it possible for the individual to undergo separations later in life and stand alone without experiencing anxiety. Losses in later life will be mastered without undue anguish and depression.

Some of the most crippled people, in a psychiatric sense, are those who have missed out on good mothering during infancy and early childhood. So many women do not realize what a great service they are doing mankind when they provide good mothering for their babies and small children. Good mothers provide the foundation within their children, boys and girls alike, upon which all else is built. Unfortunately the woman's rewards, in terms of seeing the final result of her goodness and her care, often come much later in life when her children become healthy and competent young men and women.

But unselfishness is a characteristic of the good mother; she can wait for the final realization of her rewards. Her immediate reward, which only women can have, is participating in this most vital of all human experiences—the evoking of the human spirit in the new life she has brought into the world and permeating it with her own love and goodness. Doing this will transcend in importance all else a woman can do in her lifetime. Never underestimate the vital importance of good mothering.

The Hostile and Rejecting Mother

The impact on an infant and small child of an immature, hostile, rejecting, and therefore probably somewhat unfeminine mother or, if feminine, inhibited by psychiatric disturbance, is very great. Such a mother usually will not have had a completely good mother herself. A rejecting, insecure, anxious, or hostile mother finds ways to avoid her baby. She will tend to not respond to the demands of her child.

Women who fit this pattern commonly let their infants cry for extended periods of time, leaving them hungry, soiled, too hot, or too cold. They may be unable to nurse their infants and do not find satisfaction in holding or rocking them. They often are rough in the way they handle their children, sometimes strike them, and tragically, even beat them. Very young infants can sense the stiffness and muscular tension in their mothers which is caused by the mother's insecurity and/or hostility. Infants usually react with a variety of disturbances. Unfortunately these bad experiences are internalized by the infant and young child. Instead of having internalized loving experiences with a good mother, they become burdened by an enemy within. The succeeding developmental periods of childhood will necessarily be difficult, as will be later life, for these individuals lack courage and confidence in themselves and a sense of trust in others. They tend to be vulnerable to separations and responsibilities later in life and experience excessive anxiety in such circumstances. They expect attack and injury or hostility from friendly people and in non-threatening situations. It is hard for them to love or believe they are loved, and they commonly have disturbed sexual functioning.

The Overprotective Mother

Another form of mothering which is, perhaps, not as devastating in its impact on the child as the hostile and rejecting mother but which, nonetheless, has its harmful effects is the overprotective mother. Such mothers have had the kind of infant care themselves which made them vulnerable to separations, that is, to excessive anxiety when separated from other persons or familiar surroundings. They are often beset by fears that injury or death will come to their child if they are not always close by, or they may cling to their child without a conscious reason for doing so. The overprotective attitude may be a reaction-formation (converting a feeling or a thought into its opposite) to a hostile attitude toward the child; that is, overprotectiveness masks hate. Women who envy and hate men are frequently overly protective of their male child, ostensibly for the purpose of protecting the boy. The over-protectiveness actually is a means by which they manage to fulfill their unconscious desire to diminish or destroy the male. Such mothers often treat their infants as if they were a part of their body. When a male child is overprotected he is denied encouragement and the opportunity to explore and become masterful, experiences which enhance his sense of maleness and capacity for mastery in later life.

When a woman views a child in this way there is inevitably an associated hostility toward the child. There will be a constant struggle between mother and child. The child will try to free himself and the mother will cling to him. Some women are so successful in their ability to cling to their child, particularly if male, that an excessive internalization by the child of the anxious and insecure mother occurs. Not only does the child fail to develop courage and a sense of trust but effeminacy (in the male) is also the result, in some cases so extreme as to lead to homosexuality and even the wish, in severe cases, to undergo surgical alteration of the sexual organs. Mothers of transsexuals (those who believe they are of the opposite sex) are said to have held their babies against their own bodies excessively, and when standing the baby on their laps often positioned the child's feet over their own pubic area. Overly protective mothers who cannot experience their infant and child as a separate being use their child as a means for compensating for their inner emptiness which resulted from their own inadequate mothering, and for their sense of imperfection which is derived from their belief that they are anatomically lacking or deficient because they have female genitals instead of male ones. You may find this hard to believe, but it is quite true. If such mothers had had good mothers they would have gotten over their envy of the males. Their good (feminine) mothers would have made it possible for them to realize that females are as valuable and worthwhile as males. The effects of overprotection are serious; the child's courage is less and the full expression of gender and other potentialities tends to be diminished, in all likelihood throughout the remainder of life.

In short, the effects of the mother who is not fully satisfied with herself as a woman and who is, therefore, unable to completely live out her maternal instincts and functions will be such that her child will experience some kind of difficulty achieving a fully developed manhood or womanhood. As can be seen, the effects of undesirable mothering are passed on from generation to generation.

Circumstances sometimes force such a way of life on women, but a childless or husbandless woman is usually so because of her unconscious conflicts, and their characterologic consequences have prevented her from marrying and having children. One must not, however, assume that all married parents are healthy! A high percentage are not. Later, I will discuss why some people marry for the wrong reason.

Many women should not marry, and some choose not to. Such women have had the good sense not to do that for which they are unsuited, for which they do not have sufficient interest or time to do the task well. Such women often make fine contributions to mankind in other ways, and they should never be deprecated for not marrying and having a family. Many are quite normal in the sense of not showing signs of psychiatric illness; for others it is probably the fact that they have not married and attempted to make a family that has saved them from becoming psychiatrically ill.

It is remarkable how often one sees women who devote their energies to the children of others, usually as teachers, child psychologists, child psychiatrists, social workers and the like but who cannot have children of their own or, if they have children, cannot spend much time with them. Women who find outlets for their maternalism by working with or caring for the children of others deserve our respect and gratitude, provided they do a good job. It is far better for them to live a life like this and succeed than to try to be a full-time, natural mother and fail. Not only would their life be an unhappy one, but the child they might have had is spared the effects of bad mothering and bad family life. It would be much better for those women who elect to work to face the hard fact of their limitations and forgo having children of their own.

Fathers

When the feminine woman has a new baby the father must stand by her in a helpful and supportive way. A mature man will not be jealous of his wife's attentiveness to the new child; he will freely share her with the new child, and will transmit his pleasure and gratitude to his wife in many ways. Thus the child and the mothering experience are not the sole rewards to the new mother. A baby enriches a marriage, if the couple is healthy, for both husband and wife will discover new dimensions in each other as a consequence of their increased growth with the coming of their child. Both can now discover further what maturity means in relation to the child and to each other.

It is appropriate for fathers to give some assistance in the care of the infant; however, most of the baby's care will fall to the mother. Those who think men can stay at home and care for babies and young children while the mother works outside the home are misguided. To expect a man to be able to do what Nature has designed a woman for is absurd in the extreme.

During the infant's first few months of life the man's chief responsibility is to make his wife secure. The man cannot do for the infant what the mother can do; however, she cannot do her best for the infant without a good man by her side. The strengths his own mother and father gave to him will now make it possible for the husband to provide the love and security his wife needs in order to fully discharge her responsibilities to her infant. Because the woman's energies are so highly focused on her infant, the man must attend to potentially distracting demands on her, and he must be able, for the time being, to forgo receiving much of what he previously enjoyed from his wife. He should be able to give her much more than he expects in return.

Good men have always helped their wives. It does not diminish their masculinity to take over some of the tasks that women ordinarily do when so much of her energy is taken up in the care of the new child. It is perfectly appropriate for men to do the dishes, wash diapers, and clean the house once in a while so the wife can preserve her strength. He may have to do for older children what his wife ordinarily would do. It will not hurt him to prepare meals now and then. He must bathe his wife with security, praise, and love so she can do her very best for the child. Women become irritable if they are fatigued and it harms an infant to be exposed to an irritable mother.

The father should have direct contact with the infant, too. It is very important for small babies to be in contact with their father after they have matured enough to discriminate between a mother and a father. This is especially true after the first year of life. These early experiences set the stage for both boys and girls to be able to form close relationships with the opposite sex as adults. The groundwork is laid for a heterosexual relationship. A little girl discovers intimacy with a male. The female in her is awakened, and her relationship with her mother will reinforce her femaleness. Little girls who have passed through a period of closeness with their fathers will be able to be close to their future husbands. Little boys sense something different from the mother in the father. After the boy child is a few months old the mother awakens his maleness. Being held and played with and taken along on excursions with the father reinforces the budding maleness and femaleness; which are biological givens. Nature designed it this way.

Parents Together

It is difficult to describe the quality of the experiences the infant and child can and should have with his mother and father. The child discovers that though he is separate from his parents he is known by them. There is a marvelous something which passes between a mother and child when she cares for the child; it is conveyed in her smile, her touch, her guiding hand. Fathers transmit something too, but it is qualitatively different and its effect is different in the boy and girl. The girl senses in her father a source of power and strength which permits her to be what she is, a female. The boy senses this same power and strength but in him it evokes the urge to emulate his father. The girl is designed by nature to emulate what her mother is. These are the ideals—when nature and the environment are in harmony.

It is important, therefore, for both parents to interact with their infant from birth onward; however, the mother should be the primary adult in the infant's life up to a year at least. After a baby learns to walk and begins to master the environment, the father begins to play an increasingly important part in the child's life.

Development and learning proceed at a rapid pace and the older the child gets the more he should enter the world of his own sex.

Daughters, therefore, will participate increasingly in mother's activities while sons will participate more in the father's world. Because the mother will spend more actual time with small children, it is important for her to direct their energies into play which provides suitable outlets for the little female or little male in her child which will reinforce what they are biologically. No child of either sex should ever feel (or be) ignored by the parent of the opposite sex.

Adolescence

During adolescence parents have an opportunity to undo some of the damage that was done during the child's first six years of life. Some parents mature as time passes; these are the ones who can take corrective steps. Those parents who have not improved will merely reinforce the damage that was done earlier.

With the coming of adolescence, the complexes which formed in early life become activated within the unconscious mind. The parent must move quickly and skillfully for part of normal adolescence is the breaking of family ties and eventually a physical separation from the home.

Stated as concisely as possible, fathers and sons have a second chance to find each other, thereby establishing or rounding out the boy's masculine identification while at the same time breaking the remaining unconscious erotic attachment to the mother. Girls and their mothers have the same opportunity. The parents must take the lead. The children will not, for their natural tendency is to break away. The stronger must always lead the weaker in life.

It is not my intent to discuss all of the ramifications of parenting. Many volumes would be required to thoroughly discuss the subject. It would be necessary to describe the effects of the parent's personality on the child, the nature of the developmental process in children (and in parents), how the mind works, and a myriad of other aspects of this broad subject. I wish only to focus on a few aspects of parental responsibility, in particular on parental authority and certain basic values. Authority has become a bad word in modern-day society, and evidence exists everywhere that authority is breaking down in our society and in the home. This trend is a major element in the weakening of our society.

A moment's reflection will soon lead to the conclusion that "authority" really is nothing more than a set of rules or guidelines for living. Rules, law, traditions, and values are nothing more than structures which channel the human spirit and govern conduct so that people get along reasonably well with each other, do minimal harm to themselves, and to others, and live constructively. Behind the laws there exists the threat of punishment if one deviates too far.

Ideally people should live by laws, customs, etc., because they possess within themselves sufficient authority to do so and possess an adequate capacity for reasoned thought so as to be able to comprehend the consequences when we do or do not live by the rules. Truly mature people live by the rules of civilized society because they have sufficient inner authority to do so; they do not need the police, or a threat of punishment to force them to live by the rules of society.

Not only are the rules of society breaking down, but the capacity of people to live by the rules is weakening. These facts can be traced directly to the breakdown of authority within the home, *and* to the revolutionary changes which are taking place in society's values. Remember change does not always mean progress. Life *is* ever-changing, to be sure, but change has to be studied carefully and tested before it is possible to know if the direction of change is progressive or not. Generally, changes which evolve slowly are more constructive than sudden, revolutionary changes. The revolutionary redefinition of what constitutes a family is the most alarming example I can think of. The family is the oldest and most stable organizational pattern of civilized (and pre-civilized) man, yet within a few years the word "family" has been re-defined to mean almost anything.

Parents are losing faith in themselves and in the institutions which have traditionally been the guardians of our values, namely, the church and the university. Almost any life-style can be found on or around a university campus, and its advocates within the classrooms. The churches have lost less ground, but even their certain basic human values and truths are being questioned. What then shall parents believe? And what shall they uphold to their children?

Advocating certain values to your children and expecting them to live by them is the first step. The second step is the more difficult one—getting them to follow your lead, to live by what you taught them. Here is where parental authority enters the picture. Children abide by parental authority for essentially two reasons: (1) out of love and respect for the parent and (2) out of fear, fear of rejection or punishment.

Parents who have had a good relationship with their child will have much greater success in having their children follow their guidelines on the basis of love and respect. Ideally, the element of fear should never have to be resorted to by the parent. Inevitably children test parental guidelines and authority. The art of parenting is to be able to know when to let children test new ways, and how far to let them go, and when to draw or withdraw the line.

In general, parental authority has deteriorated badly in our society. No clearer evidence of this exists than the push to make it possible for minor children to sue their parents. No one endorses parental abuse of children, and no effort should be spared to protect children from physical and psychological abuse. However, when parental authority is destroyed, the child is *also* abused. Those who have not internalized parental authority are unable to live by society's authority.

It is imperative, therefore, not only for the sake of the child's personality development, but also for the sta-

bility and growth of society that parents again exercise
benevolent authority with their children. I cannot possibly describe in detail how far parents should go in the
exercise of authority. The principle, however, is a clear
one. Set the ground rules for living and expect them to
be followed. Parents should be consistent and always try
to present a unified position to the children. Do not let
the children play one parent against the other. Have no
hesitation in using the phrase "I say so" in response to
your child's defiant "Who says so?" Do not fear a clash
with your children. Life cannot be lived without confrontation.

Parents should listen to the child's point of view and
if the child is right, then change course and go his way.
But if not, then hold firm, and if a confrontation develops, do not be afraid of it. I have seen some extremely
intense confrontations between parent and offspring.
Emotions ran high, but eventually the child recognized
that the parent was right. Almost without exception a
better relationship developed between parent and child
subsequent to the confrontation.

Remember President Truman's low popularity with
the public when he stood firm on certain national and
international issues. Now most people respect him deeply
for being strong enough to take a stand and make good
the phrase—"The buck stops here." Your popularity with
your child may temporarily drop quite low, but later it
will be very high. You will be promoting personality
growth in your children, building their character by being a loving authority.

Chapter Three

Sons

By approximately the age of three a child begins to experience his maleness or femaleness in the form of a strongly possessive, loving, and sexual interest in the parent of the opposite sex. It is *normal* for children to experience these feelings and emotions. This period is referred to as the oedipal period. If the child does not get over these feelings but submerges them into his unconscious mind we refer to this as the "Oedipus complex."

While it is true that children can experience sexual excitation toward the parent of the same sex, while being bathed for instance, it is unlikely that the sexual and romantic interests toward the parent of the same sex ever reach a fraction of the intensity of that which is felt for the parent of the opposite sex. The outcome of the Oedipus situation is dependent upon the child's earliest experiences with its mother and, of course, the events which occur simultaneously with its budding sexuality.

The resolution of the oedipal situation is crucial for mental health and for the successful living of life. If resolved in the proper way, life will go well; if not, much can go wrong and much disappointment, failure, mental illness, and tragedy may be the result. The effects on a person's life as a consequence of the success or failure to resolve this developmental phase can influence one's

41

values, character structure, and sexual identity. They
may determine whether one becomes heterosexual or
homosexual, perverse in one's sexual behavior, a failure
or a success in one's life work; they may influence the
choice of a life's work, vulnerability to psychiatric illness, self-destructive life patterns, even the kind of person one chooses to marry; the consequences really are
far-reaching. This period is a very crucial time of life.

For the Oedipus situation to be resolved, correct behavior must be forthcoming from the parents. First, the
parents must be mature, and this implies the absence of
sexual identity disturbances. The father must be a mature man and the mother a mature woman. Second, the
parents must love each other and have established a
strong marital bond. The parent of the opposite sex must
tactfully reject the child's romantic overtures but not
the child. Above all, the parent must not respond seductively.

Many women do respond seductively toward their
sons; often these are women who were overly protective
during the boy's earliest months of life. Mothers who
reject their infants also behave seductively toward their
small sons. Such behavior entices the son and often pro-
longs the oedipal period indefinitely. Seductive and/or
possessive mothers tend to make confidants of their sons
and thereby make it apparent to the boy that he enjoys
a special place with his mother that his father does not.
Such mothers often enter into secrets with their sons
and openly exclude the father. These excessively close
and clandestine arrangements whet the boy's appetite
and keep his unconscious hope aflame that he may indeed someday win his mother as a love object. Abnormal
mother-son relationships may extend into adulthood so
that not only is there a failure to resolve the original
oedipal attachment to the mother, but the excessive continual maternal input into the boy's personality profoundly affects his subsequent personality development.

A good mother will continue to interact warmly with
her son during the oedipal period and will in no way
make him feel guilty or ashamed because of his strong

and sometimes overt expressions of love for her, but she, in subtle and tactful ways, will make it increasingly clear to him that he can never reach his romantic and sexual objectives with her. Such a mother will not feel threatened or embarrassed by her little "lover." It is sometimes necessary for very small children to sleep with their parents when they are frightened or ill, but when the child enters the oedipal period it is better for him to sleep in his own bed unless, of course, he is seriously ill. A night or two in bed with mother and father does no harm under those conditions.

Mothers should not permit their little boys to watch them dress and undress or bathe, or sleep with them all night when the father is away. Warm embraces at bedtime and on other occasions are necessary and important so that the little boy can experience his male sexuality and love, but these encounters must not be too prolonged and they should never be associated with behavior on the mother's part which leads the child to conclude that he has a special place with his mother to the exclusion of his father.

The parents should not conceal their affection for each other but, at the same time, excessive displays of romance such as embracing, fondling, etc. between his mother and father can dampen a small boy's spirit. A boy's father would try to balance the boy's interest in his mother by spending time with him, teaching him how to do things, and by taking him with him whenever possible. It is also important that the boy, mother, and father do things together; this permits the boy to discover that there is a way for him to be together with his mother *and* father without the inclusion of his romantic and erotic interests in his mother occupying the forefront of his attention. During his struggles with his "love affair," the boy's mother and father must stand by him as tolerantly and solidly as ever; this makes it possible for the boy to eventually discover that though his romance is a lost cause he has his mother and father as solid allies forever.

Another aspect of the boy's oedipal situation is the feeling he also has for his father. He loves his good father but unconsciously (and at times consciously) hates him to the extent that he wishes his father were dead so that he (the son) might have mother all to himself. Naturally, when filled by such strong hostility there is also a fear of retribution by his father. Strong fear and guilt form as a result of his erotic love for his mother and his love and hate for his father. It is the mixture of love and hate toward his father that is the primary source of guilt, the bulk of which becomes resolved in the course of time as he gives up his erotic longings for his mother. As these wishes disappear, so does the hate for the father, and with it the guilt goes too.

Associated with the hostility toward his father, the little boy develops a special type of fear about which there has been much speculation by psychiatrists regarding its origin.

Despite the absence of any such direct threat from his parents or other adults (some parents *do* make such threats) the boy develops the notion that because of his sexual interest in his mother, his father would castrate him were he to find out. An incredible belief indeed, but one which probably exists in the unconscious minds of all boys. Boys do realize some people do *not* have a penis and testicles (women) and it is probable that their immature minds cause them to reason that someone removed them, possibly as a punishment. The castration fear can become quite intense in unfavorable family circumstances and, if not overcome, adds a powerful and harsh component to the child's developing conscience. His sense of fear and guilt may be quite profound and have serious consequences for his further development, as will be explained momentarily.

Having normal parents who are a regular part of life, the boy gradually overcomes his oedipal wishes, guilt, and fears, including his castration fear. Feeling secure (because his good mother from his earliest period of life lives on inside him) he will grapple with his feelings within himself and about his parents. By means of continuous interactions with his parents he will eventually discover that the only way out of his dilemma is to give up his mother as a romantic and sexual object. Good memories of the mother of the oedipal period are formed which reinforce earlier ones. Simultaneous with this realization the boy will have been strengthening his relationship with his father and overcoming his fears. The process of identification with his father now goes into full swing; the son will eventually become fully identified with his father and the world of men.

Coincidental with these realizations, he will have made new discoveries having to do with his father which are a source of deep satisfaction. His father will not have been standing idly by during this period; he will have been forming a solid, enduring, and guiding relationship with him. Eventually the good father will take his place by the good mother's side within the mind (personality) of the boy. The experiences between father and son can be magnificent indeed.

It is difficult to put into words and adequately describe the process by which the father fills his little son's personality; that is, how the process of identification with the father takes place. There is a natural affinity between father and son which is loving but not romantic or erotic. In addition to the many times the boy observes his father from a distance and during his daily experiences with him, by means of which he acquires some of his father's traits, values, and so on, there are special and exquisite moments (I am recalling experiences with my own three boys) which occur when father and son are alone together. During these fine moments good feelings pass between them, but much more occurs; the one personality—spirit if you will—passes into the other. The father fills his son with his spirit. A stillness comes for a moment or two; the transience of life may be apparent, but at the same time there is a sense of permanence. The father is taking his place within the personality of the son; he will remain there forever. This process by which the father is incorporated into the personality of the son is a continuous process, but when father

and son share special experiences, such as working together, good conversation, climbing a mountain together,
etc., the process is rapid and intense. As you can see, it
is imperative that father and son know each other. This
cannot happen unless they spend time together, and a
lot of it. Physically, the father will someday be gone, but
he will live on indefinitely in the personality of his son
and stand by him solidly like a rock.

The boy is willing to pay a price for such experiences
with his father, the price being the giving up of his
romantic interests in his mother. Son and father are no
longer divided by the woman. All three are now together
in ongoing life and father and mother exist side by side
within the personality of the son. He has now acquired
two strong and faithful internal allies who will stand by
him the remainder of his life. He has set sexuality aside
for the time being. When he is older, and physically and
psychologically mature, he will find a woman of his own.
With the firm backing of both of his parents (within
him) he will succeed in forming a loving, sexual, and
fully committed relationship with a woman.

During the processes of giving up his romantic and
sexual attachment to his mother and identifying with
his father, the boy's castration fears will gradually die
out. With his sexual interest in his mother rapidly disappearing, the basis for his castration fear has been
removed. As a consequence of such a fortunate resolution of his oedipal situation the boy does not form a
severe conscience. His behavior will be more in keeping
with his own conscious wishes and needs and the expectations of the environment rather than the demands of a
tyrannical conscience.

It can be clearly seen what a vital influence the father is during the early years of a boy's life. There is no
adequate substitute for a good father during this period.
Good fathering requires effort and time. A quick hello, a
few minutes or an hour a day with the son is woefully
inadequate. Father and son need to *know* each other
and discover the rewards of being together, and particularly of cooperation with each other. A father should

take his son with him when running errands, etc., with, and at times without, the mother being along. Father should teach son elemental skills required for life, thus increasing his capacity for mastery. They should play together as well as work together. They should be close friends, but the father-son distinction should never be lost.

Father will, by necessity, be an authority figure who establishes rules and sets limits. The boy will discover that it is to his advantage to live by these, and he will realize that his father's rules are not unreasonable and that his own effectiveness in society will be greater if he lives by his parents' rules. These remarks should be understood in the context of each person's uniqueness; that is, the degree of parental authority offered by healthy parents leaves ample room for the son to find ways for fully expressing his own personality.

In those circumstances where the son may have been endowed with talents or intelligence greater than the father's (or mother's), or where the environment offers opportunities which were unavailable to the parents, both parents should encourage their child to go on to greater heights. A good father (or mother) will never be jealous or envious of the son's greater abilities or opportunities; rather, he will take pride in them and help his son reach these greater heights.

During the oedipal period when the boy will be experiencing intense competitiveness toward him, the father should never fall into the trap of responding in kind. Instead he will show the boy that he wants him to go as far as he can and that he, the father, will help him get there. There is no basis for competition between them. In short, a successful resolution of the oedipal situation, which includes the boy's identification with his father (father's masculinity), does *not* mean the boy will limit his level of achievement in adult life to that of his father. Quite the opposite is true. Because the father and son are not competitors, since there is no (or very little) guilt and fear in the boy toward his father, the boy is free to progress as far as his natural and acquired abilities can take him; he will feel the reassuring presence of his loving father inside of him for the rest of his life.

It is one of the marvels of nature how the boy will, under proper conditions, ultimately identify with his father instead of his mother when he has been reared by normal parents. He also acquires other human qualities from his father besides a reinforcement for his biological masculinity. Courage, fairness, gentleness, strength, integrity, etc., are taken on from the father too, but there are certain other very special qualities which he should develop from his relationship with his father. From his strong father he will learn how to stand firm when it is necessary, and how to be masterful. The mother encourages him on to mastery and the father teaches him how; from both he acquires the strength to stand firm, to take a position, to be committed.

From having been reared in this way, and as a result of having witnessed the daily living patterns of his parents, he will have seen his father in the rightful place of every married man—at the head of the family. He will have seen the mutual respect and love between his parents and he will recognize that father had the final responsibility for the family and that he was the final authority. Boys who have been reared in an ideal family never fear women, or other men for that matter; they can form intimate and fully satisfying heterosexual relationships, and they can enter into cooperative relationships with men. They can form strong bonds with other men because they not only have no fear of them, but there are no unconscious hostile, competitive, or homosexual fears they must guard against by remaining distant from other men.

Abnormal Complex Solutions in the Boy

It can easily be imagined that the physical absence of a good father during the years three to six (and later) can have far-reaching effects. Fathers die, are sent to war, or are taken away excessively by their work responsibilities. If the boy is fortunate enough to have a good mother she will not attempt to make up for the absent father by intensifying her relationship with her son. She will, instead, attempt to find substitute fathers for her boy and manage her own needs for a man in her life in a way which is appropriate to her own life situation. Boys with mothers like this tend to do rather well if they have some exposure to good men. Often a grandfather, uncle, neighbor, teacher, etc., will be having a much greater effect on such a boy than they or others realize. Boys with absent fathers soak up the attention and interest of men who are not their fathers. Mothers without husbands should always encourage such relationships for their sons.

The worst thing that can happen to a boy (and girl, which I will discuss later) is to have a passive, effeminate, and ineffectual father who either overtly or unconsciously hates, rejects, and competes with him and who is dominated by his wife, as all such men are. It is this marital pattern which I truly believe is the primary pollutant of the human spirit, of the couple themselves and particularly of the children who are born into such families. The consequences for mankind are extreme. The marvelous experiences which characterize good family life are denied the children. Instead of gradually giving up his mother as a romantic and sexual love object, the son will be driven even closer to her by his hostile and rejecting father. His mother will gladly comply with his needs, for in addition to some degree of natural protectiveness which she may have for her son, she can fulfill her own needs for closeness to another human being by means of her son. Furthermore, she may cling to him as if he were a possession, even a part of her body. Women who marry effeminate and/or passive men have never fully developed their femininity; they may be colorless and inhibited, or more often are aggressive, domineering, and often masculinized. Some may seem feminine but this is usually a sham for they may be skillful manipulators or they may be frightened little girls. These women often use their sons as a substitute husband of sorts. Their possessive and dominating behavior with their sons provides them with the opportunity to subtly emasculate the male even though they are their own sons. As was noted earlier, such women always unconsciously (and sometimes consciously) hate, envy, and fear men. The boy has many strikes against him. In addition to the bad maternal influence of his infancy period, there is no way he can resolve his oedipal situation and rapidly forming oedipal complex.

The boy's castration anxiety will never be extinguished nor will his strong erotic attachment to his mother. He will sense his father's hatred for him, a perception which, along with his castration anxiety, will cause him to fear men for the rest of his life. He will form a tyrannical, harsh conscience and a warped personality. Thus the absence of a genuinely feminine mother early in life, who should have filled him with self-confidence, courage, and trust, plus his excessively close tie with his domineering and probably somewhat masculinized mother will inhibit him further. In addition to these factors, the presence of a hostile, rejecting, passive father who fails to provide a strong male identification object forces the boy to become passive and/or feminine in his personality makeup. There is no alternative but to remain tied to his mother and thus he is forced into submissive identification with her. He may show some elements of her aggressive personality but more commonly he will be passive. He will also internalize his passive father, but instead of having acquired an ally who stands beside him he will have acquired a second enemy within (the first being his mother), both of whom constantly threaten him and make him a frightened, ineffectual male. Passive and/or effeminate men always have an unconscious unbroken romantic and sexual tie to their mothers. As you can see, there are vast empty places in the personalities of boys who have been reared in families like these. Lacking are the encouraging, good, and bountiful mother; the good, loving, and strong father with whom he eventually identifies; and the memories of happy family life wherein the father was the head of the family, and so on. These empty places have great relevance for self-help endeavors and for psychiatric treatment, as I will show. These basic deficiencies must be comprehended and dealt with in order for self-help or for treatment to be successful.

Variations in the Childhood Development of Boys

I have described two opposites in child development, one ideal and the other extremely abnormal. What follows are brief descriptions of some modifications in these extremes.

The most common form of childhood development of boys is where both parents are reasonably normal but where both are also burdened by some degree of neurosis, that is, unconscious conflicts of their own. The mother may not have become masculinized but is only unsure of her feminine identity, her role as a new mother, and her responsibilities. The father may have some residual castration anxiety and oedipal conflicts in his unconscious mind. He may be only mildly passive, or he may be quite masculine but may tend to avoid his family responsibilities, in particular his relationship to his son. Sometimes the father is quite normal but circumstances may take him away excessively, as is frequently the case with hard-working and successful professionals, businessmen, and military personnel. In family constellations like these the child may resolve his oedipal situation to some degree; however, there will remain some attachment to the mother. Castration anxiety is never completely extinguished, guilt is somewhat excessive, and identification with the father is never fully achieved. An inhibited masculinity is frequently the result. Efforts at mastery are always attended by anxiety. Success may be achieved in life, but with greater effort and more anxiety than necessary.

Boys who never fully resolve their oedipal situation and who do not overcome the associated castration anxiety experience difficulty cooperating with others. For them cooperation means personal submission, an experience which (in their view) confirms their passivity and violates their sense of maleness. They resent, and find it difficult to accept, suggestions, advice, or help from their fathers or other men. To do so is to admit weakness, smallness, and acceptance of submission. Such boys are constantly at war with themselves. They continue to strive for the full expression of their masculinity, potentialities, and abilities, but they cannot do so because of their unconscious conflicts.

The effects on the development of a boy when the mother is remote or absent vary, depending on the time in the child's life when the influence of the mother is removed. If the mother dies or deserts the boy in his first few years of life he will suffer from lowered courage and self-confidence. Others, including the boy's father, can make up the deficit to some degree but these influences can never equal what the natural and feminine mother can provide. These boys will find it difficult to love a woman and may suffer sexual disturbances. To be able to experience intimacy as an adult depends upon having experienced closeness to a feminine mother.

If the mother disappears during the height of the oedipal period of the child's life, resolution of this conflict becomes impaired or impossible. The child retains his unconscious ties to his mother. There invariably is a depressive cast to his personality resulting from the loss which he usually fails to mourn. If he is fortunate enough to have continued to have a loving masculine father in his life, his male identification will take place but he will not be fully prepared to form a heterosexual relationship when he reaches manhood. Substitute mothers provide some opportunity for such a boy to work out his oedipal conflicts but I doubt if this is ever done fully. The consequences on a boy's life of the loss of a mother who dies during the oedipal period (if she was a feminine woman) are different from those if the mother deserted him. Mothers who desert their children by simply walking off, or through divorce, have invariably had a negative impact on their children from birth on. In some instances the boy is better off if such a mother does disappear; to continue to fall under her influence does more harm than having a substitute mother who may be more feminine and loving. The point here is that women who do not succeed at marriage have usually failed as mothers to some degree.

There is a difference between women, and their effects on their sons (and daughters); those who are forced by circumstances to work outside the home soon after the birth of their child, and women who voluntarily go to work. The latter group uses work as an escape from their maternal responsibilities. Ideally, such women should be helped so that they can stay at home and be mothers. When this is not possible, it is probable that the child is better off with a surrogate mother than to be exposed all day to a mother who neglects it or is anxious, irritable, or depressed while attempting to carry out her maternal responsibilities.

Some Consequences of Abnormal Development in Boys

It is a marvel that boys who grow up in seriously disturbed family circumstances ever succeed in life upon reaching adulthood. Those who do, usually have had parents who were not extreme in their own character pathology. Many do fail in one way or another, as will be described in the section on why people fail. One thing is certain, such men make poor husbands and fathers; many should not be fathers. This may seem like a harsh statement, but after having seen over the course of twenty-five years the effects of such men (and the women they marry) on their children, I am completely committed to the view that they should not be parents.

Men who have had childhoods of the kind I have just described nearly always marry dominant and aggressive women, if they marry at all, or they may become homosexual. It would matter less what kind of woman they married if they did not have children. I have known couples who were not mature men and women as I have defined them who worked out a satisfactory marital arrangement and who had the sense to recognize their inability to ever be good parents. I admire such people who have the strength of will to avoid bringing children into the world. They choose a variety of occupations; some are ballet dancers, others hairdressers, designers of clothing (and they defeminize the clothing of women and feminize the clothing of men), often they work with food. If well endowed intellectually, and if they are exposed to an intellectual environment, they tend to choose the humanities, the social sciences, psychology, philosophy, art, and so forth, instead of the hard sciences and professions where they must be precise, committed, authoritative, and responsible to a high degree. There are exceptions, of course.

After having chosen these professions or vocations, some of these individuals do mature as a result of their exposure to the responsibilities associated with work, and with family life if they marry. This can happen if the family patterns in which they were reared were not too pathological and if in the course of their lives they were fortunate enough to be associated with friends and associates who matured them; that is, from whom they received part of what they missed out on as children.

One cannot infer with certainty the nature of a person's early childhood by the kind of life's work chosen; however, the trend I described is there, and quite definitely so. As an example, pilots, whose responsibilities are great and who must be precise, committed, and courageous, have different personalities, as far as I have been able to tell, from many of the men who choose psychiatry, psychoanalysis, psychology, and social work; where there is ample room for tentativeness, less demand for accountability for their actions, and a high degree of personal safety. Weak men cannot survive in exacting professions and occupations.

Some of the most unhappy men I have known are those whose early development caused them to enter fields of endeavor which prevented them from fully developing their masculinity and, therefore, from achieving their full potential. I recall a priest who entered the

priesthood in his early years because of his fear of women
and guilt about sexuality. Later his masculine and paternal urges almost overwhelmed him, and he finally
became deeply depressed because his life was unfulfilled.

Chapter Four

Daughters

Good mothering is as essential for the girl as for the boy. Having had good mothering during the first three years of her life, the little girl can, like the boy, face subsequent developmental stages and later life with courage, trust, and self-confidence. The obvious should be stated: a fully feminine mother values a little girl as highly as she values a boy. This estimation of femininity will be transmitted from mother to child in a number of overt and subtle ways from birth on. The little girl will gradually achieve a psychological separation from her mother but will continue to internalize her good mother just as the boy does. Both boy and girl may resent weaning but the other gratifications mother provides and her tactful, nontraumatic (gradual) method of weaning will prevent it from being a trauma in the life of the child.

Like the boy, the girl will experience certain sexual excitations in relation to her mother as a consequence of the care she receives, but these experiences are of minor importance if the mother is a good feminine mother. At about the same time the little girl's femininity causes her to become erotically and romantically attracted toward her father, for whom she develops a deep attachment. She is now confronted with complicated developmental challenges during the period from age two-and-one-half or three to six. During this period her hostility toward her mother has two roots; she blames her for her lack of male genitals, and she is her rival for father's affections. Recall how little girls play mother with dolls and how ardently they become mother's little helper when a new baby arrives. What is not so obvious is the wish in their unconscious minds to have a baby by their father; the wish for a baby from her father replaces her wish for a penis. This progression is normal and is evidence of the blossoming female in the little girl.

It is important for the father to ignite these wishes in the little girl but he should never be seductive toward his daughter so as to fan these fires too much. Just as a seductive mother who forms too intimate a relationship with her son has a bad effect on him, so too does a seductive father have a bad effect on his daughter. Such fathers usually do not have a fully satisfying marital relationship with their wife. Eventually the little girl must face many disappointments; she is denied a penis, a baby, and her father's romantic love. These are bitter disappointments for her to overcome. A happy outcome for her depends on both a feminine mother and a masculine father who have a solid marriage.

Mother and father will stand by her reassuringly if they are mature. Mother's appreciation of her own femininity and the world of women begins to have its effect on the girl. Father's respect for the mother, his love for her, and his high estimation of females in general reinforces the little girl's appreciation of her own gender. The girl realizes she cannot drive a wedge between her parents and finally she no longer wishes to do so. Her identification with her mother proceeds smoothly and she will become a feminine woman. She will internalize good memories of her strong father, who loved her and regarded her so highly and protected her, but she will not identify with him, just as a normally developing boy will not identify with his mother although he retains loving and reassuring memories of her within him. The girl unconsciously will come to realize that she will have to delay finding a male and that her baby will come from her relationship with him. A girl who develops normally will be able to love a man, experience intimacy with him, and cooperate with him. She will be a fine wife and mother when her time comes.

The Effects of Poor Mothering and Poor Fathering on the Girl

The little girl whose mother is absent or who rejects her or deprecates her, overtly or covertly, must find security somewhere. Such mothers are usually domineering, aggressive women, or may be neurotically inhibited. The girl may be fortunate enough to have another woman near her, or if her father is present she will inevitably turn to him for the nurture she should be receiving from her mother.

The husbands of such women inevitably take over some of the mothering of the child out of a sense of compassion for their child. This usually begins when the little girl is quite small. Sometimes men do this because of their identification with their own mother. They find a part-time maternal role more comfortable than paternal responsibilities. Finding most of her security from the father early in life instead of from the mother introduces a serious complication into the development of the girl. Instead of being filled with a good mother who forms the basis for her courage and self-confidence, the small child takes in a poor substitute (the father) and one which, along with the influence of the imperfect family in which she will grow up, will prevent her from developing a self-confident feminine personality. Instead of having a good mother inside, which forms the foundation upon which all else in her personality and life will be built, there is a male there—and usually a weak one at that.

Later, during the oedipal phase when the little girl's romantic and erotic sexual interests for her father appear, this early attachment and internalization of her father is powerfully reinforced (the mechanism of which I will soon describe), the combined effects of which lead to a very profound "father complex" and frequently a masculine identification which is extremely difficult for the girl to overcome. The resolution of her very early and her oedipal attachment to her father is virtually impossible because of the personality of her mother— that is, her rejection of her own feminine identity (or inability to fully express it) and of her maternal responsibilities. Mothers like this who are inhibited or domineering, aggressive, and/or withdrawn and remote, do not draw the little girl into the world of women, and they provide a very unsuitable model for the child as a person with whom she can identify. Some identification does take place, and this complicates matters even more; the little girl now adds unfeminine or aggressive and domineering qualities to her personality.

It can be said with complete certainty that when a girl does not overcome her penis envy, her oedipal attachment to her father, and her identification with him, that she lacked the courage to do so because she failed to receive adequate mothering from the beginning of life onward. Persistent penis envy and masculine identification of any significance is always associated with an unbroken erotic tie with the father and some degree of identification with him. Had the girl been filled with more courage, and had her parents been mature (fully feminine and masculine) and fully committed to each other in a satisfying relationship, she would have discovered that her best solution lay in becoming fully female. It may come as a surprise to you, but it can be said with absolute certainty that women who do not overcome their penis envy and their identification with their father are basically afraid to be female and are, therefore, afraid of an intimate relationship with men. Guilt, too, plays a role in their turning away from femininity. It derives from the oedipal period when mother was a hated and feared rival and competitor.

Women whose childhood development followed the line I have just described are always divided within themselves. They are biologically female, they have gotten just enough from their environment to develop some degree of femininity, but they did not get the adequate mothering that makes it possible for them to become fully feminine and mature women. Some girls retreat entirely from the challenges of the oedipal period and revert into a dependent tie with their mother and remain infantile and sexless adult women; others, of course, become very masculinized.

Women whose childhood development did not proceed along reasonably normal lines are destined for much trouble in their later lives. Psychiatric problems may appear during childhood; however, the most common times of disturbances are at puberty and when they attempt to marry, and especially when they become mothers. Some become homosexual; frigidity is a common problem. They have difficulty getting along with other women. Their marriages often fail because they compete with and diminish their husbands and cannot experience closeness with them. Some never do marry, avoiding men altogether; others have repeated affairs and may eventually marry only to have the marriage fail. They choose men who are weak, passive, and ineffectual when they are able to relate to men. Some who do marry and have children fail miserably as mothers; they tend to feel well until their baby is born and suffer depression or some other form of illness after its birth. The sense of loss is great after the baby's birth, as is the guilt about their rejection of the baby, or their effort to be a mother. For them the baby is a forbidden product of "incest."

Many women choose careers, often selecting those usually filled by men. I think it is quite probable that the so-called "liberation" so many women are seeking actually reflects a flight from the responsibilities only a woman can discharge; hence, women's liberation attracts many of these women. Worst of all, if they do marry and have children, they perpetuate their illness onto the next generation. It is tragic that such women ever become mothers. Life begins with the mother and its ultimate outcome for men and women alike rests to a large extent squarely upon that foundation of courage and confidence, of real solidity which *only* a good mother can provide. The evidence for this assertion is overwhelming.

The Effects of Absent Fathers on Little Girls

When a little girl has a good, feminine mother but loses her father during her oedipal years her future growth is complicated. Unless there is an older brother or some other adult male in or around the family she will be denied the impact of a powerful growth-promoting stimulus. Her sexual instincts will not have been evoked by a male and as a consequence she will not be fully prepared for a close heterosexual relationship as an adult. In families where there was a father but one whose work responsibilities took him away excessively, the maturation of a girl is somewhat impaired. The presence of a strong father provides the security for the girl to develop her femininity.

I believe it is imperative that mothers in such situations find a means by which their daughters can interact with a good reliable, solid man. I recall a woman patient whose father was killed in combat prior to her birth. When she was in grade school the children teased her about not having a father. She came home crying and told her mother. As it happened the mother's future husband was there. He swept this heartbroken little girl up in his arms and said, "Yes, you do. I'm your father."

She told this to me amidst her sobs as she expressed her gratitude. His presence in her life had a profound, positive impact on her subsequent development.

Chapter Five

Living Successfully with Failure

The principles which explain why people fail in life and why they become psychiatrically ill relate directly to the developmental processes which were discussed in the preceding chapters. Success implies finding a way to fully express one's capabilities and potentials, to be able to live by the dictates of reality, and to contribute constructively to life. There are certain times and certain situations which are commonly related to failure and to emotional illness.

Abnormal childhood development leads to the formation of unconscious conflicts which are termed "core" or "nuclear" conflicts or complexes because of the time of life when they are formed and the pervasiveness of their effects. Core conflicts have powerful effects on personality and behavior and much of a person's outlook on life, the values he lives by, the nature of his likes and dislikes, his choices, his character, and life-style. The most common unconscious conflicts are: excessive dependency, separation anxiety, guilt, excessive and unextinguished castration anxiety (in association with unresolved romantic and sexual attachment to the parent of the opposite sex), and penis envy (in women). Related to the latter two conflicts are those which cause cooperation to be confused with submission. These conflicts or complexes, and others, lie unresolved within the unconscious mind and function like chief executives issuing commands which distort the individual's view of life and prevent him from making it what it could be.

Living with One's Core Conflicts and Complexes

Having acquired certain kinds of character traits and values which fall short of those of mature masculinity or femininity, and by living a style of life which is harmonious with those traits, a person may escape overt mental illness. This is an extremely important point to understand. For instance, a woman who never overcame her penis envy or her childhood romantic attachment to her father may function rather well in a career as long as she avoids attempting to form an intimate and/or lasting relationship with a man. So long as she avoids men her (core) conflicts can remain dormant in her unconscious mind. She may even substitute homosexual gratifications for heterosexual ones or she may avoid sexuality altogether. A man may remain symptom–free (of psychiatric illness) as long as he strives only for a modicum of success in his work rather than trying to get to the top. Some persons may marry and effect a reasonably harmonious adjustment provided they pick a mate whose character structure blends with their own. For instance, an aggressive and dominant woman may pair off with a passive man, and as long as they do not strive for the kinds of marital adjustments which characterize a healthy marriage they may remain relatively symptom-free.

In other words, persons who are bedeviled by unconscious conflicts and the products of these in their personality do manage to find a "fit" in their occupations and interpersonal relationships of a kind which does not activate the core conflicts that are stored in their unconscious minds. These persons do not live as fully or richly as men and women can, but at least they achieve an equilibrium within themselves and with their environment. Millions of people must be living constricted lives and never fulfilling themselves. If these "fits" were never disturbed there would be far fewer mentally ill and obvious life failures.

For most people, however, life does not remain static; the "fits" they find in the environment become disturbed. There is an inner push, a physiological trend toward maturation in the first few decades of life. Such physiological changes can be seen most clearly in childhood, at puberty, and early adulthood. Social pressures of many kinds are brought to bear upon the individual which push him on to maturity. The most common of these pressures are those which bring the opposite sexes together. There is a natural attraction between male and female, despite abnormal childhood development which may tend to keep them apart as adults, and it is a social convention for the sexes to mate. There are unexpected promotions, and those which are struggled for. Men are suddenly confronted by unplanned military service which catapults them into positions of heavy responsibility. Society and Nature cause men and women to make families even when they are psychologically unsuited for such responsibilities. Some children are planned for; others are conceived because they are "supposed" to occur after marriage; some come by accident.

One way or another environmental forces eventually impinge on individuals and push them into ways of life which characterize greater maturity and a deeper involvement with, and commitment to, life. There usually is enough "health" within individuals to make them want and attempt to mature and live a more involved and committed life. The degree of health and strength within the individual determines how far he can advance without failing or becoming psychiatrically ill. However, this very process of deepening one's commitment to life in the direction of greater responsibility and maturity activates unconscious core conflicts which, in turn, cause people to fall ill or to fail. This is a fundamental principle.

The Environment as a Trigger of Unconscious Conflicts: An Overview

Adolescence and early adulthood have long been recognized as times in life when illness breaks out and personality begins to malfunction. The emotional strain causing this has several sources. There are hormonal changes which awaken sexuality. In addition to this source of pressure from within, the youth must begin to break his ties with his parents and, perhaps most significant of all, he begins his efforts at establishing a relationship with the opposite sex. There are usually new work responsibilities as well. The confluence of these pressures demands that the youth change in many ways. Close inspection will show that the new responsibilities and opportunities are not themselves overwhelming or stressful. A new job usually is not so complex; a lovely girl friend is not a source of actual threat. Giving up one's childhood relationship to one's parents and anticipating leaving home or actually leaving home is cause for grief; however, this detachment is usually gradual.

The true sources of the young person's anxiety, depression, or more serious illness are the core conflicts within his unconscious mind, his efforts to involve himself more deeply with his environment trigger and activate these. The presence of the member of the opposite sex toward whom there is a romantic and sexual interest mobilizes or activates the repressed unconscious conflicts which are a residue of the unextinguished romantic and sexual interest once experienced by the child toward the parent of the opposite sex. Those romantic and sexual interests were forbidden and were associated with castration anxiety, and guilt in relation to the father or, in girls, guilt in relation to the mother. The girl who is the object of the young man's interest is not, therefore, experienced simply as just a young woman. There may be an excessive awe felt for her, love far out of proportion to the situation, that is inconsistent with the boy's knowledge of the girl's actual qualities. These are feelings which betray, along with his anxiety and/or other symptoms, the presence of unconscious conflicts.

Once having had their unconscious core conflicts awakened through their efforts to establish a heterosexual relationship, some young people retreat from such involvements permanently, some for long periods of time, and some persist in their efforts only to become seriously ill. Those young people who resolved their childhood romantic and sexual ties to their parents do not form core conflicts; they are successful in these efforts as young adults.

Those who are fortunate enough not to be too heavily burdened by unconscious conflicts and who possess greater strength of personality will persist in their efforts to form a heterosexual relationship and achieve success. Some persons level off at this point and live a pattern of repeated love affairs but are never able to take the next step into marriage. They may experience love for the opposite sex but promptly drive the other person away when marriage becomes a real possibility. Those persons who live such a life pattern choose lovers who themselves are not psychologically ready for a marital commitment.

Once marriage has occurred, many kinds of maladjustments and overt psychiatric illnesses may appear for the first time. The point is that maladjustment, and certainly illness, is not caused by a lack of compatibility of interests, but caused by the effort being made to live intimately (lovingly and sexually) with a person of the opposite sex. The unconscious conflicts and their representative character traits are the bases of the trouble. Couples in trouble often try to explain their marital disharmony as incompatibility. Actually, they may have a great deal in common and love each other.

Many marriages fail at this point if the balance in one or both persons is greater toward sickness than health; that is, if the unconscious forces are great and get out of control. The troubled person does not realize that the true sources of his unhappiness, provocative ways, symptoms, etc., lie within himself.

It sometimes happens that the awakened unconscious conflicts become silently resolved during these turbulent times. Once awakened and mobilized, mature forces within personality can have a neutralizing or resolving effect on them. This, of course, is the happy and desired outcome. Young married couples should never divorce immediately when trouble begins because they may resolve their unconscious conflicts through the process of living together. Unfortunately, many marriages end in divorce at this point.

A less favorable outcome, short of divorce, is one which leads to an empty life. Many married couples establish a safe emotional distance from each other, thus permitting their unconscious conflicts to recede further into the unconscious mind. They may rarely express love for each other; sex will be rare or perfunctory; each will cultivate his own interests, and so on. Any effort to reintensify and deepen their relationship will promptly awaken unconscious conflicts; symptoms may appear or, more commonly, the couple will begin to do battle again. Fighting creates emotional distance between them once more.

Some married couples achieve a happy relationship before their first child or subsequent children are born. The balance of health is generally greater in persons who have been able to reach this level of marital commitment without becoming ill or "incompatible." A new baby serves as a powerful maturational stimulus for both the woman and the man, more at first for the woman, or if the unconscious conflicts are mobilized, illness may result.

In the woman, unconscious conflicts which resulted from insufficient nurture by her own mother may be awakened by her attempts to nurture her infant. Regardless of the nature of the unconscious conflicts which are triggered by the birth of the child, it is these and not the child itself which are the bases for the illness and malfunctioning in the mother.

The young mother's efforts to live out her more feminine responsibilities will also trigger those early conflicts from her infantile and childhood period. In short, with the formation of a family a triangular situation (two parents and a child) will have been created; this constellation awakens the conflicts associated with the original childhood triangle. A woman with a new baby often pushes her husband away as if he were the forbidden (father) male, and the husband reacts with hurt and anger. Some women feel complete at last when they possess a child, particularly a boy child, and they may exclude their husbands from their lives.

Men react symptomatically to the coming of children too. Many cannot accept the responsibilities of parenthood. To do so means unconsciously taking the father's place; that is, the unconscious wish to destroy the father and take his place with mother has been reawakened by having become a parent. There are men whose unconscious sense of guilt associated with these conflicts is so great that they dissociate themselves nearly completely from their families. Some withdraw angrily from their wives because they receive less "mothering" when a child is born.

Work is another trigger which awakens unconscious conflicts. Interestingly, work outside the home is less a conflict trigger for women than for men. Work for women provides a means for escaping from the feminine responsibilities of homemaking, motherhood, and being in an intimate love and sex relationship with a man. These are the predominant conflict triggers for women. By working the woman creates environmental conditions which permit her unconscious to lie dormant.[1] She will be successful unless her feminine and maternal urges are too strong. When this is so, work becomes less satisfying; she will seek a heterosexual relationship and try marriage, and at this point begin showing signs of psychic distress. Sometimes the work situation will awaken unconscious conflicts too, particularly if she must work with other women. Unconscious conflicts formed in early life with the mother can be awakened by a female supervisor, or a male supervisor may evoke a woman's competitiveness towards males.

Working recreates the role of the breadwinner for the male. Some men can work well provided they do not attempt to follow their father's vocation or profession. To attempt to do so recreates, symbolically, the early wish to take the father's place within the family by destroying father and possessing mother. This unconscious conflict may be so profound and pervasive that success of any kind is impossible. To succeed at anything amounts to doing something forbidden. It is remarkable how intensely anxious or disturbed some men become when they are on the brink of success or have succeeded. Some men may achieve minor successes but become increasingly disturbed as their promotions increase, even though they are perfectly competent and well-prepared for their new responsibilities. Many highly gifted, well-trained, and experienced men cannot function well when their level of success becomes too great, especially when their success threatens to push them into a top executive position.

Persons whose core conflicts have not been resolved often cannot remain symptom–free in the presence of their parents. Young people usually try to avoid their parents as a means by which to permit their unconscious conflicts to recede more deeply into their unconscious. Some young people may place geographical distance between themselves and their parents, believing that to do so will lead to a greater degree of personal comfort. Some children never achieve a friendly adult relationship with their parents. For example, a man's unresolved attachment to his mother creates excessive discomfort within him when in her presence, and his hostility, fear of, and guilt toward his father precludes a friendly adult relationship with either of his parents. Furthermore, sons sometimes believe they are subjugating themselves and losing their individuality when they enter into a friendly adult relationship with their father. The same formulations apply to adult women and their mothers.

Case Examples

What has been written can be made more vivid by means of brief case examples. These may help you detect signs in yourself and in your loved ones of failure and/or psychiatric disturbances, and increase the likelihood of your taking the necessary steps to ensure success and/or freedom from illness.

Preadolescent Children

Many young children develop transient symptoms or even severe illnesses. These, of course, require as great care as those of adolescents and adults but there is a first rule for disturbed young children that must always be looked into. When a child becomes disturbed, look first at the parents and into the family situation. Straightening out the trouble there frequently leads to improvement in the child and even to recovery from illness. When improvement in the child does not result, then professional help should be sought for the child. I will not discuss the various forms of psychiatric disturbances young children are known to develop but, rather, limit myself to the following statement. Because a disturbed child nearly always reflects a disturbed environment, first look into aspects of the child's environment.

Adolescence

It is not my intention to describe all of the myriad forms of upheaval young people may show during this period. Instead, I will focus on the main causes of failure to adjust to life. Some young people cannot do well in school or will fail in their efforts to hold down a job; however, the main reason illness occurs in adolescence is the demand (biological, personal, and social) that sexual role definition occur, and that relationships with the opposite sex be established.

When family life has not led to the kind of experiences for the child which I described in earlier chapters, young people have difficulty crystallizing their gender and sexual role, and have trouble forming meaningful (meaning close and intimate) relationships with the opposite sex. Without the internal psychological conditions

which good family life during infancy and childhood lead
to, the individual is ill–equipped to live up to the demands of a mature adjustment with a member of the
opposite sex.

Case No. 1: This young woman, one of two children,
was a normal-appearing young child. Her father was a
passive man and a problem drinker but successful at his
work. When she was very small she seemed to derive
more comfort and nurture from her father than from her
mother. An aggressive woman, her mother was always
active and busy with community affairs, openly demeaning her husband throughout the girl's early life. A brother
was born when the girl was five-years-old. At the age of
eleven or twelve the patient became extremely rebel-
lious. Although promiscuous with boys, she could never
form an enduring relationship with one. While still in
her teens she entered into an overt homosexual way of
life, rejected offers of help, and eventually became a
confirmed homosexual. She will never change but has
instead aligned herself with the gay liberation movement.

Case No. 2: This patient was described as a beautiful
infant and a feminine little girl. Graceful and likable,
she performed well in school and in dancing. Her outgo-
ing personality caused her to be very popular through
high school. Her father was a very weak man who lacked
the capacity to be an authority figure; her mother was
dissatisfied with her role as a woman. At age fourteen
the patient became enamored of a much older man and
went so far as to sleep with him. She could not date boys
her own age. In college she had affairs with much older
men but finally settled into an overt homosexual way of
life. She had previously associated with a series of extremely unsuitable men, being capable of nothing more
than transient and meaningless affairs, a pattern which
continues despite several attempts at treatment.

The mothers of these young women have had the
greatest difficulty in fulfilling their roles as mature
women, mothers, and wives. Of equal importance is the
fact that the fathers were weak, passive men. Having

grown up in such families, these girls could not develop in a way which permitted them to become self-confident and feminine, and capable of forming meaningful relationships with the opposite sex. Their efforts to do so triggered their unconscious conflicts, forcing them to flee from heterosexual relationships and accept a homosexual way of life. Take special note of this family pattern. Wherever it exists the children from such a marriage inevitably have some form of psychiatric disturbance.

Case No. 3: This man grew up in a family where the father was a hard-working, conscientious and successful man, but one who was distant from his family. As a result the patient never had a close relationship with his father. He was very close to his mother, however, and spent a great deal of time with her throughout his growing-up years. He observed a constant antagonism between his parents. He was popular in school, did well and achieved certain goals, being spurred on by his mother without his father's involvement. He first noticed psychiatric symptoms when he attempted to form relationships with women. The more determined his efforts became to succeed in his relationships with women, the more severe his symptoms became. These included anxiety, depression, somatic complaints, and impotence. He has never been able to form a successful heterosexual relationship despite treatment.

Case No. 4: This patient showed signs of psychiatric disturbance from early life on; his symptoms included neurosis and nightmares. His father was successful but a remote person in the home and a man who was dominated by his wife. The patient's mother could not function as a mother to him during the first few years of his life but later developed a very close relationship with him. With the arrival of puberty the patient began drinking heavily, got into physical fights with his father, and could not successfully date girls. After several years of a marginal adjustment he began to date a woman several years older than himself, promptly began drinking heavily, and deteriorated severely in his overall life adjustment. His treatment failed and he eventually committed suicide.

The case examples are of young men who had not resolved their unconscious romantic and erotic attachment to their mothers. Their mothers had been too close to them, their fathers were weak or remote, or both. Some of these mothers were seductive and possessive. When these boys entered adolescence they could not, in a figurative sense, distinguish a girl friend from their mother. The effort to find closeness with a girl awakened (triggered) the unconscious unresolved erotic ties to the mother, the associated guilt and fear of the father; thus the only thing to do was to take flight from the girl in one of several ways. Case No. 3 avoided the opposite sex forever. Case No. 4 acted out his unconscious conflicts by physically fighting his father and dating older women. His desperation finally drove him to suicide.

Aside from the personal suffering all of these examples experienced, such individuals, and there must be hundreds of thousands just like them or worse, become somewhat of a liability to society. This is not meant to sound harsh or critical, for these are sick people who need and deserve treatment. Men and women like these, who eventually marry, perpetuate their parents' family pattern by way of their own personalities and those of their spouses.

You will have noticed, I am sure, that the family patterns of the patients referred to in the preceding vignettes were far from ideal. Had the fathers of these young people been strong men and the heads of their families, and had their mothers not been dominant and so aggressive and/or so ineffectual in the mothering role, these people would never have become patients because they would never have formed the unconscious (core) conflicts which later made them ill.

Many young people who were reared in less than ideal family circumstances do form relationships with the opposite sex. However, they tend to pick mates who blend with their own disturbances. Passive boys choose aggressive girls or, more commonly, aggressive girls pick passive males. That is, the girl takes the initiative. Those incapable of really close relationships with the opposite sex choose partners or mates who are agreeable to a distant relationship. Their conflicts continue to lie dormant under these conditions. Some make relationships with the opposite sex in a way which poses no threat. This can be seen most clearly in persons who experience sex role blurring. Relationships often remain platonic. There are relationships of love but no sex, or it is all sex but no love. In the unisex type of relationship, the relationship possesses some aspects of humanness, but it is neutered so that gender and sexuality hardly enter into the picture at all. Sexual differences and interpersonal commitments are less, and as a consequence unconscious conflicts remain untriggered, with the result that these persons experience less anxiety or other disturbing symptoms.

Some avoid the opposite sex for life. They may date but never marry, or they may be entirely celibate. Some persons take flight from heterosexual relationships and enter homosexual relationships as a consequence of their first brush with heterosexuality.

The point to be grasped is that when a young man and woman form a relationship this should be a step toward a richer and more rewarding life. When young people avoid the opposite sex, or when they develop emotional disturbances as an outcome of their efforts to form a heterosexual relationship, unconscious conflicts are present which have been triggered by the closeness to the member of the opposite sex. These conflicts produce the psychiatric symptoms.

When a young girl becomes masculine or extremely prim in her character style, or shows other signs of a rejection of femininity, this is a sure sign that she is in psychiatric trouble. If she has only girl friends and/or picks older women for her friends, especially if these women are somewhat masculine, parents should be alerted to possible trouble in their daughter. Discovering their daughter to be homosexual is cause for great alarm, for homosexuality is a major psychiatric illness which requires the most expert treatment. Do not listen to educators and mental health professionals who say homosexuality is normal. It is not; it is a manifestation of illness.

Boys who fail to date and who have only males for friends, or who have no friends at all, are usually in psychiatric trouble. It is good for boys to have strong bonds with other boys, but when they avoid relationships with girls something is wrong with them. Effeminacy in an adolescent boy is evidence that he is not developing as he should. Young men and women frequently use drugs as a means for quieting the anxieties which are aroused by their attempts to form a relationship with the opposite sex. Drug usage is, of course, cause for great alarm and immediate intervention. There are many other signs of illness young people show.

The trend in many young people toward drugs, noncommitment, and "doing their own thing" is a gigantic example of human failure. Theirs is a protest against convention; it is not a constructive alternative to the ills of society but a self-defeating and destructive one. Their movement reflects disintegration, not evolution on to higher human values. Their advocacy of the use of drugs, their music, their heterosexual relationships (which are fluid, transient, uncommitted), are clear signs of personal psychiatric illness which is offered as a social norm. But these people cannot be blamed, for they are the product of family life and a society which ill prepared them for the responsibilities and rewards of a mature life. Understanding the causes of this phenomenon does not excuse it. Parents should take the strongest possible stand when they see their children enter into these ways of living.

Marriage

Many young men and women successfully manage courtship and are able to marry. To be able to do so usually reflects a greater degree of emotional health. Males and females were meant to mate, and when they do (marry) this can be taken as a sign of greater health. This is not always true, as some of the following vignettes will illustrate; however, the very fact that a couple can marry suggests both are capable of a deeper commitment to the opposite sex than those who cannot take this step.

Some couples are capable of marrying and remaining free of psychiatric disturbances even though both are heavily burdened by unconscious conflicts. This can be explained in several ways. Although they are married, the relationship may not be very intimate or intense and thus unconscious conflicts are not triggered. Both may have been strong enough to keep unconscious forces in control. What is very common are those marriages where neurotic (unconscious) factors of the couple blend, the most common example being that of the aggressive, more dominant woman who marries a passive, weak male. As long as nothing upsets the balance of healthy and sick forces in each of the partners in relation to the other, the marriage may survive and neither will become manifestly psychiatrically ill and marital harmony may endure. Sooner or later the balance usually becomes disturbed, however, by the coming of children or by a gradual building up of dissatisfaction. Those who marry very young frequently do so for neurotic (unconscious) reasons. Fifty percent of these marriages end in divorce.

Case No. 5: This man had been reared in a family where the father had been a steady worker but he was a passive man; the mother had been the primary figure in the patient's life. The father had been away for many months during the patient's early life. Upon his return to the family the patient's mother became chronically ill and the patient's care fell to others. His mother and father never had a good marriage. His own signs of disturbance appeared soon after his first marriage. It was his excessively close relationship to his mother, and the absence of his father, which led to the formation of unconscious conflicts which eventually destroyed his marriages and caused him to fail. The patient himself was rather passive and he married an active, aggressive woman. Severe incompatibility erupted almost immediately. Two children were born but the marriage ended in divorce. The patient began an affair early in his marriage and after the divorce he married the woman of the affair. After his second marriage his behavior continued to deteriorate; he did poorly at work, drank, took drugs, had numerous somatic symptoms, and was unfaithful to his wife. He became overtly homosexual for a brief period. He behaved ineffectively in relation to two additional children who were born to his second wife. He eventually required hospitalization and later committed suicide. This was a very serious illness; the outcome of which might have been different had he received treatment earlier.

Case No. 6: This woman became ill soon after her marriage. Her mother was an aggressive, domineering woman and her father was weak and passive. She met her future husband while still in high school and dated him on and off for many years before marrying him. She had a brief romance with a man twice her age shortly before marrying her boyfriend of long-standing. After marrying she began having somatic complaints, was irritable, troubled by fatigue; there was marked marital discord. When her babies arrived she was unable to care for them, relegating their care to hired help. She eventually resorted to severe alcoholism, divorced, and remained unmarried. Good treatment at the time of the affair with the older man, when she married or when the children arrived, might have saved her.

Case No. 7: This young woman was the product of a fairly successful marriage; however, her mother was a very socially active woman who was clearly made uncomfortable by having to stay in her home and be completely responsible for the care of her children. The patient carried on two courtships simultaneously. One man was stable and reliable; she loved and respected him. The other was less reliable but more sexually exciting. It seemed she could not find a man who embodied the qualities of each. She married the stable man, soon became depressed, there was much marital discord, and divorce ensued. She was later successfully treated and was able to marry again.

The parental family patterns of those who become

disturbed as a consequence of marriage are much the same as those who become disturbed when they first attempt to form a heterosexual relationship. The fathers are either weak, passive, remote, or absent. The mothers are usually aggressive or more dominant than their husbands, and all have faltered or failed to some degree in the role of mother and, of course, wife.

Many who marry attempt to find satisfactions outside the marriage which they cannot find with their spouse. The most common form of this is infidelity. Infidelity sometimes occurs as a vindictive act against the spouse who fails to participate fully in the marriage by avoiding loving and/or sexual intimacy with the spouse. The unconscious conflicts are usually oedipal in nature; that is, the man is unable to express his sexual wishes with the basis for infidelity by the wife. When a man and woman cannot fully express themselves with each other there is usually something in their unconscious minds which stands in the way.

Greater affluence, and greater permissiveness within the home and in society, have caused young people to view marriage as a less serious commitment than in times past. Loneliness appears to be a powerful motivation which causes people to marry prematurely. Unfortunately, many young people are not ready for these commitments. Faced with the challenge of making their marriage work, they take flight instead. Unfortunately, children are born to many of these marriages that eventually fail.

Parenthood

Of all the commitments of life which precipitate psychiatric illness, parenthood ranks near the top, especially for women, who cannot escape the responsibilities of being a parent, as can the man by going to work every day. The coming of children usually reflects a deepened commitment of the man and woman to each other. In addition to this change, the child (or children) forces each into clearer sex-role definition. A family has been created. The child, the clearer sex roles, and the family constellation itself trigger unconscious conflicts which

cause many people to become ill and many families to
break up. This is human tragedy and the consequences
can be extreme for the individual and for society. The
forming of a family can be, and for many is, the happiest
time of life; for others it is a time of tragedy and heartache.

Case No. 8: This young woman was one of many
children. Her father was alcoholic, an unsteady worker,
a remote figure in the home because of his own passivity
and involvement with other women. When at home he
was an emotional man who was overly affectionate with
his children, particularly his daughters. At times he was
covertly seductive. Despite his characteristics, his children felt closer to him than to their mother, who was a
harsh disciplinarian and the dominant figure in the
household. Her daughters, including the patient, never
felt close to her.

The patient married and for the first few months of
the marriage she was quite happy; then she became
pregnant, had a child, and promptly became depressed.
She developed fears (phobias) of the dark, and could not
stay alone because of her fear that someone would break
into her home and rape her. She became frigid, found it
impossible to be pleasant to her husband, and eventually became so provocative that divorce was becoming a
probability. This woman's unconscious conflicts were resolved by treatment. Her health was restored, and her
marriage was saved. She subsequently had a second child
without a return of her illness, a happy outcome indeed.

Case No. 9: This patient's father died when she was
a very small child and her mother had followed a professional life which is usually exclusively a male profession. The mother and grandmother were dominant, aggressive women. The patient had much difficulty forming heterosexual relationships but finally managed to
marry. The marriage promptly dissolved after she in-
sisted upon an abortion. Many years later she married a
fatherly man but could not become pregnant. They
adopted a child but she became acutely anxious and
could not care for it. After a few years she left her hus-

band, lived a very unconventional life and finally, after several years, rejoined her husband at his insistence. She promptly became severely ill and required hospitalization. The marriage ended in divorce. This woman's life course could only have been constructively influenced by the most expert doctor. Such a woman should never attempt motherhood.

Case No. 10: This man was the product of a marriage where the mother was volatile, emotional, and overly anxious about her child. The father was a successful businessman but he was completely dominated by his wife. The patient was mildly depressed most of his life but he managed to marry and have several children, though he had little to do with them. Furthermore, to be successful as a provider for his family proved to be difficult for him. His is a very common pattern. Many such men can (and do) become good husbands, providers, and fathers if successfully treated.

Fewer men seem to become ill after becoming a parent, probably because a good portion of their day is spent outside the home. Some, however, become acutely ill, others withdraw from their families, and others become unreasonable in their behavior toward their offspring and spouse. I am referring to jealousy toward the child, overt hostility, competitiveness, or withdrawal. Fathers can withdraw from their families and thereby avoid acute psychiatric illness; to do so permits their unconscious conflicts to recede more deeply into their unconscious minds, and they are no longer manifestly ill. Women cannot escape their children as readily and as a consequence they become mentally ill; their unconscious conflicts are constantly triggered and mobilized and illness results.

Thousands of women like the few examples given do just what these women did—they give up part or all of their family. By breaking up the family they escape the conflict-triggering situation which had mobilized their unconscious conflicts. Divorces and/or abandonment of children are acts of desperation on the part of the sick person. They are frantically attempting to ease their anguish, anxiety, depression—their suffering—and to regain their health.

Some women promptly relegate the care of their child or the children of their growing family to others and go to work in order to get away from the responsibilities of being a full-time mother. When they are less exposed to these responsibilities their unconscious conflicts can recede more deeply into their unconscious, their psychological defenses get put back together, and they may be relatively symptom-free. I have known many women who are relatively symptom-free when they are away from their children, but when they try to be full-time mothers they become ill again.

The signs of impending failure of the marriage are easy to detect. Instead of pulling together, the husband and wife begin to provoke each other and fights ensue. The man often withdraws from his growing family. He may become jealous of the attention his wife gives his children. Such a man never received enough mothering as a child; as an adult he wants it from his wife and feels cheated when his children get her care. Presently the wife finds herself having to shoulder many of her withdrawn husband's responsibilities. Then the children are deprived of her care. She becomes more resentful, and complains and criticizes. The husband withdraws more. He may start to drink, find a mistress, or spend more time at work than necessary. The wife is overworked, lonely, and she begins to expect too much from her children in the way of gratification and attention. Finally comes the divorce.

The coming of a family can serve as a tremendous stimulus to the maturational processes of men and women. I know an example of how the adoption of a child precipitated a severe psychiatric illness. When the childless woman is less ill but just sufficiently troubled by unconscious conflicts to be unable to become pregnant (psychic infertility), the adoption of a child may promote maturation in her. In such cases a woman who for years has been unable to become pregnant can have children of her own after she has adopted a child. I believe what happens is that since the child is not her own there is less unconscious meaning attached to it and she can become a mother. Actually caring for the child mobilizes her unconscious conflicts so that the healthy aspects of her personality can resolve them. Furthermore, she has mastered the new situation and matured as a consequence. Some women, strangely, can keep their families intact and remain symptom-free so long as there is no man in their life. Many such women wrongly assume the man himself is causing the trouble when they find that they are less troubled when he is away. It may not be the specific man to whom they are married at all, but the presence of a male who triggers the woman's unconscious attachment to her father and her competitiveness toward men.

While parenthood appears to be more of an illness-producing life situation for women, work is more so for men. Men may be miserable at work if circumstances have forced them to work at jobs which they hate or for which they are ill suited. Being ill suited for a vocation can produce chronic strain and in severe cases a mental breakdown, and certainly will often produce poor performance on the job. Work is usually illness-producing and/or the cause for maladjustment because of unconscious conflicts. The individual may be well suited for his life's work, may like what he is doing, and yet fail to function well enough even though he has all of the skills necessary to succeed. The practical significance of this fact is that one should not immediately change jobs when signs of distress appear. To do so might be a serious mistake and one based on the false assumption that one is not suited for a particular job. The real basis for the difficulty often will be found in the person's unconscious mind.

Case No. 11: This young man admired his father while growing up, but his father was unable to form a close relationship with him. There was an undercurrent of jealousy in the father toward his son because of the son's very close relationship to his mother. The father was an exacting man, stern and yet devoted to his family, but from a distance. The marriage of this patient's parents was not a good one; there were long periods of coolness between them; the family could rarely be together on an outing without tensions arising. The patient never broke his strong infantile ties to his possessive but somewhat cold mother, and later he clearly remained too deeply attached to her.

He married young, having picked a very aggressive and competitive woman, and soon this couple had a child. The patient exhibited extreme jealousy toward his son, thus driving the boy excessively close to his mother. This fact made the patient all the more jealous and hostile toward his wife and son. The marriage survived, however, but life took a marked turn for the worse when he attempted to succeed at a life's work for which he had prepared himself. At this point frank signs of mental illness appeared which severely complicated his chronic maladjustment with his family. He went progressively downhill in his overall life adjustment, failed at the work for which he was extremely well suited, and had to be hospitalized. The marriage ended in divorce. This tragic outcome might have been averted had a good doctor treated him.

Case No. 12: This patient was symptom-free and had been able to marry and have a family without apparent difficulty. He supported his family, saw military service, but then joined his father's firm. He soon began to show signs of anxiety, to use alcohol, and began to conduct himself at work in such a way as to cause his superiors alarm. When he was informed he was being groomed to take his father's place as president of the company his behavior took a sharp turn for the worse. He had to be hospitalized. This man had many strengths, and it should have been recognized that taking his father's position would trigger off his unconscious conflicts.

Case No. 13: This man came from the typical family which leads to the formation of unconscious conflicts in the children. He hardly knew his remote, harsh father and was excessively close to his mother. He married but had a very difficult time holding his family together. It was largely through his wife's efforts and encouragement that he managed to hang on. He received a promotion and was able to purchase a nice home for his family but he kept his family isolated from the neighbors. He became increasingly anxious, and began being preoccupied about religion. He went through a series of so-called religious conversion experiences during which he believed he heard God telling him to give up his work, leave his family, and devote his life to religion and the ministry. He did devote his life to religious work, but fortunately for him his wife obtained professional help for him before he abandoned his family.

The principle to be grasped in these examples is that commitment to work (or school), the wish to master the environment, serves as a trigger of unconscious conflicts. These, in turn, cause the individual to fail, to become manifestly psychiatrically ill, or to suffer unnecessarily from anxiety, anguish, or depression.

Some men are able to achieve success but then promptly ruin their careers by behaving in self-destructive ways. They make bad decisions which force their superiors to replace them; they bankrupt their businesses; they disgrace themselves; and some become severely ill with typical psychiatric illnesses. Others fail before even achieving much success.

While work alone frequently serves as a mobilizer of unconscious conflicts and the precipitant of illness, work is often associated in the man with being the breadwinner for his family. This combination of being successful as a family man and at work becomes a very powerful conflict trigger. It is the position as head of the home, the family, and success at work which triggers unconscious conflicts which, in turn, prevent the man from being successful in the male role.

At one time in every little boy's life, as I outlined in the chapter on childhood development, his maleness is aroused by his mother and he wishes to succeed with her in a romantic and sexual way. These wishes usually disappear in the course of normal development, but when they do not they are associated with profound guilt. When the repressed childhood wish to succeed with the mother is never extinguished, the guilt associated with this wish can become awakened by efforts to succeed later in life. In other words, every success becomes equated with the childhood wish to succeed with the mother (in the case of boys); all success then becomes impossible, especially highly important ones. Some men can be successful so long as they do not try to succeed in the father's field of endeavor. Others cannot succeed at anything they try. These differences can be accounted for by the strength of the unconscious conflicts.

Hundreds of thousands of people go through life destroying themselves. Common ways people harm themselves are: provoking others on whom their success depends, making faulty decisions, accidents, alcohol and other drugs, and failure to seize upon opportunities which clearly present themselves. Many go through life making partial successes but never getting as much out of life as would be possible for them to achieve.

A common time of difficulty for women is the realization of the lifelong dream of having the kind of home they always wanted. Just as receiving a long wished-for job or appointment can serve as a prime conflict trigger for men, so, too, can the house of her dreams become the prime trigger for a woman and cause her to falter when she finally obtains it. These should be times of joy, and are in healthy people, but they become illness-producing (anxiety, depression, overt psychosis, provocative behavior, etc.) in persons bedeviled by unconscious conflicts.

Not only do many women begin to fail or show signs of illness in connection with moving into their dream house, many others attend poorly to their homemaking responsibilities. The same unconscious conflicts are usually the reason for this. To do well as a homemaker has for them the unconscious meaning of competing with their mother, outdoing her, and being more pleasing to the father. Their guilt associated with the old and repressed childhood wishes prevents them from doing their best as wives, mothers, and homemakers. This is why so many women go to work soon after having a child.

Males frequently avoid overt mental illness by never grabbing hold of a life's work. Such avoidance is a mental mechanism whereby the individual protects himself from the conflict-triggering effects of commitment to life. The perpetual male student is an example. Some of these men fail to succeed when they finally leave the status of student. Women do this too; however, they do it differently from the way males do. Women may use work as a way of avoiding marriage and a family, and thereby avoid an illness. Work is much less of a conflict trigger for women than for men. The reason for this is very simple and obvious. By working the woman avoids a way of life (making a home) which would trigger her repressed childhood wishes to replace her mother in the home with her father.

The most glaring example of the mechanism of avoidance is the scores of young people who cannot make mature heterosexual and steady work commitments. They frequently live on parental subsidies or work just enough to survive. These are lost persons whose way of life can be explained by looking into the childhood period of their lives. Some social psychologists and sociologists claim social forces such as rebellion against war, society's assault on the environment, etc., are the bases for their way of life. There may be some truth to these claims, but it is overwhelmingly true that these people missed out on good family life during their childhood years. The inability to work, the self-defeating rebelliousness against *all* conventions, the blurring of sex roles, the inability to make heterosexual commitments, their reliance on drugs, their music and dress, tell a clear story.

Loss and Reversals

This is a broad subject, and loss poses a challenge for all persons many times throughout life. You will have observed that up to now I have described life situations that provoked varying degrees of illness (symptoms, behavior, feelings, etc.) and malfunctioning by virtue of the individual coming closer to his life experiences. The greater degree of commitment and involvement, the increased responsibilities, triggered the unconscious conflicts which caused failure and/or illness. Now we will discuss the opposite—separation, loss, reversal. Here the individual must give up that which was important or dear to him. Such experiences can also trigger unconscious conflicts.

It has been shown that persons who suffered sudden and/or harsh separations and losses during early life are more vulnerable to those kinds of experiences in later life. This is another reason why the continuity of the child's relationship to his family should not be interrupted during his early life and growing-up years. Reactions to losses in later life can be severe and their effects extremely far-reaching. Some people become depressed and never really come out of it and remain totally or partially incapacitated for the rest of their lives, although most depressions eventually clear up.

It is difficult for young children to mourn their losses; they frequently never do and as a result a depressive quality forms in them which persists for years, and at times for life. Later losses and separations, which in themselves would be manageable, may produce anything from low-grade to severe depressive reactions. For these reasons—not to mention the negative effects on the overall personality development—those forces in society and within the individuals themselves which cause women to abandon their very small children, usually by going to work, through divorce, or simply through neglect, must be dealt with somehow. Fathers must not neglect their children either. This is another reason why I make such a strong plea for the integrity of the family. It is our most precious social institution, yet in many ways it is the least protected and supported. A small child who has to separate from his mother every day when she has to leave for work is being traumatized and made vulnerable to the stresses of adult life, particularly loss.

The women's liberation movement, and others who advocate relegating the care of small children to others so the mothers can go to work, are giving very unsound advice to mothers. This is a very bad aspect of that social movement. The mother should be a constant and loving figure in the lives of her children when they are small. When she separates from them every day she is forming a core of separation anxiety in them and a vulnerability to later loss and separation.

Once children are in school all day the mother can then spend this time in other ways; it does not matter so much where she is when children are in school, provided she does not exhaust herself and have nothing for her family in the evening. It is important for mothers to be at home when the small children come home from school. It is a very rich experience for the child (and for the mother) to be greeted by a loving mother. It is deplorable that economic conditions have forced so many women to abandon their infants and small children. The importance of constancy of parents for infants and small children cannot be overemphasized.

Some physicians and researchers believe they have noted a relationship between early loss (during childhood), a subsequent loss in adulthood, and then the subsequent development of somatic disease, including cancer. I believe this is probably true although, obviously, not everyone who has suffered losses will develop cancer—there are other factors at work, too. However, losses that are not fully mourned can lead to a chronic state of resignation which probably increases vulnerability to invasion by radiation, tars, viruses, and other possible carcinogens.

Looking closely, one observes that each day involves some losses which are imperceptible. The most common one is the rapid rate at which one's children grow up. It is, of course, a source of pleasure to see them grow but it is a cause for sadness too. The years race by and all of a sudden children leave home. Some people react depressively to this event and may become severely ill and remain so for a long time.

Parents who have turned excessively to their children for love and attention, often to the exclusion of meaningful and satisfying relationships with others, including their spouse, are subject to depressive reactions when their children leave. These are the clinging, possessive parents who have wanted to get from their children rather than being able to give to them. A transient sense of loss and depression or sadness is normal when children leave home, but such a reaction should not persist.

Death of a loved one often precipitates depression of major proportions. The relationship to the loved one may have been too exclusive; there may have been no one else the depressed person loved, or the lost person may have been unconsciously hated as well as loved. The death, then, is in part a wished–for fulfillment and produces extreme guilt which accounts for the depression.

The principle to be understood is that the richer the early life, in the sense of good mothering and good fathering, and the fewer the traumatic separations and losses, the better will be the capacity to manage losses, separations, and reversals in later life. This is because the later loss does not reawaken the earlier one; it is also because there are rich past experiences to fall back on during the transient period of emptiness when a loss, a reversal, or a disappointment has occurred. These are stored resources to draw upon in such times of need. Furthermore, those who have had a rich childhood not only have the capacity to mourn their losses but they also have the personal strength to form new relationships with which to replace the lost ones.

I suspect the reason very old people dwell so much on the past is not only because there are central nervous system changes which destroy recent memory but because their lives become increasingly empty as they age. To be continuously aware of the emptiness in their ongoing lives could lead to much anguish, despair, and depression. Remembering the rich past is a way of avoiding being alone, a way of replacing the inevitable heavy losses of old age. This illustrates again how important a rich childhood is.

Case No. 14: This man lost his mother when he was a boy of six. It came as a sudden shock; one day his mother was no longer there. She had been an extremely gentle and loving mother, bountiful in her capacity to give love and nurture. She had taken great pride in her boy and had encouraged him to be competent and masterful. His father was a masterful man who was equally proud of his son, and though the boy lost the continuity of the family at the age of six the foundation for his personality had been firmly set.

This boy was fortunate enough to have a number of women relatives to replace his lost mother. Despite this fact he became acutely aware of the transience of life, of his aloneness. At times he would cry uncontrollably. These experiences occurred more often when he was alone on long summer days or nights, or after parting from relatives whom he had visited. As a man he was unusually sensitive to human tragedy. Parting from friends always seemed like permanent separations; it seemed that he would never see them again. Sunsets tended to haunt him. The intense presence of life during springtime sometimes created an acute awareness of his own separateness from all living things around him, and with this awareness there was a strong longing for something. When he became a physician he was very careful with his patients for the preciousness of life was ever in his consciousness. It was not until thirty years later that he finally adequately mourned his mother's death during his own psychoanalysis. As a result, separations from loved ones became much more tolerable; the sense of mystery about life preoccupied him less. The effects of loss after the age of five or six are much more readily overcome by treatment than losses before that age. Very early loss more seriously disturbs personality development.

Case No. 15: This woman was the product of parents who were far from ideal. The mother was an inhibited, rejecting woman, yet the patient grew up very closely tied to her mother. She had been a tomboy, and prepared herself for a professional life but married before she worked in her field. She admired her husband but was very competitive with him too. She never got along well with her own daughter but was very close to her son. When the son left home for college she became severely depressed and had to be hospitalized. It took several years of intensive treatment before she was free of her depression. This woman viewed her son as a possession, as a part of herself, and as a means for being close to another living being in order to make up for the good mothering which was missed in her early life. Without treatment such women as this often become chronically ill with either somatic or more classical psychiatric illnesses.

Acute Physical Trauma

Physical assaults on the body, or sudden threats to life, may serve as conflict triggers while also being stressful in their own right. A very common example of this are the acute psychiatric disturbances which follow major surgery. These usually clear up rather quickly as physical health is restored. It is probable that the stimulus deprivation which is often associated with surgical aftercare plays a part in these illnesses. It is well known that nonspecific stimuli from the environment play a part in maintaining normal mental functioning.

The insult to the integrity of the body can awaken unconscious castration anxiety which is the true basis for the psychiatric illness. Sometimes separation anxiety plays a part too, for in a sense the patient undergoing surgery is very much alone despite the constant and expert physical care he may be receiving.

Depressive reactions are extremely common following a major medical or surgical illness. There may be direct chemical effects on the brain from the toxic byproducts of the disease, but the most probable basis for the depression is the loss aspect of the illness. Major illnesses separate the individual from his loved ones and from his usual surroundings. The temporary nature of life may become very clear; death may have been close at hand.

It is probable that anyone could be forced into an illness by extreme stress. Mental breakdowns during combat are examples. People do get worn out from overwork and begin to malfunction; some may collapse totally. However, psychiatric investigations have shown that even in many of these patients unconscious forces have been triggered by the threat to life or by the chronic exposure to harsh conditions.

Usually, however, psychiatric disturbances result from an interplay of everyday environmental factors and unconscious forces. The responsibilities associated with maturity are the triggers, the situations, which mobilize unconscious conflicts that are the true or ultimate bases for the illness. Illness-triggering events may be acute and unusual, such as surgery, but they usually are the responsibilities of everyday life. Psychiatric illness may appear when young people start dating; following or in anticipation of marriage; after marriage; the making of a home; and the coming of a child or children. Attempting to be successful at work, promotions, the successful achievement of a life goal, or attempting to follow the father's footsteps may make men ill.

Losses are a major cause for psychiatric illness. Illness may vary from mild depressions to psychosomatic disorders, to severe depressions, and at times to suicide. The sense of loss can be caused by changing jobs, moving from one home to another, leaving home, children growing up, children leaving home, job reversals, separation from loved ones, deaths, withdrawing love from a previously loved person or place, growing old, seeing loved ones grow old, failing physical health.

Where illness has resulted from a progressively deepened involvement with some aspect of the environment, or a greater degree of commitment, or the intention to make a new commitment, the natural reaction is to separate from the conflict-triggering, illness-producing situation. It may be necessary for certain severely ill persons to shed their responsibilities and even detach themselves from their many involvements. To do so may even be lifesaving. However, for many the degree of psychiatric illness may not be that great, though painful. For these, it is much better in most instances not to withdraw from the situation but to remain involved. Remaining involved keeps the unconscious conflicts mobilized and if the mental strain is not excessive or too prolonged, conditions are right for maturation to occur. When there are supportive elements in the environment and the opportunity to periodically retreat for brief periods, the chances for maturation to occur are increased. One should never quit unless he absolutely has to.

Chapter Six

Guides to Maturity

Persons who are failing can achieve a more successful life adjustment without the benefit of professional help through self-help. The primary focus will be on married couples whose marriage is not bringing out the best in each and, as a consequence, is not providing the best possible home life for their children.

A basic assumption upon which the guidelines that follow are based is that men were meant to be masculine, that women were meant to be feminine, and that when this is so a harmonious heterosexual relationship is possible; these qualities reflect a central aspect of health. Therefore, despite what happened to the child during his early years which may have adversely affected his personality formation, I believe there is an inner trend toward maturity and health, and an attraction for the opposite sex. This is self-evident. Nature, then, is our greatest ally in the quest for a happy and successful life. My purpose is to describe ways for giving Nature the best possible assistance. What follows is a "do-it-yourself" manual for achieving personal change without going to a psychiatrist.

I believe that efforts at self-help can change one's habitual ways of behaving, believing, and feeling; and even resolve unconscious conflicts. When more mature ways of behaving are achieved, unconscious conflicts are usually triggered and mobilized so that the healthier aspects of personality can resolve those conflicts which underpinned the old ways of behaving. These periods of change are often accompanied by anxiety or depression, often by a great deal of dreaming, and even a transient outbreak of symptoms.

The most effective psychotherapy deals with the outward manifestations of personality and their counterparts in the unconscious mind. That is, we try to link unconscious meanings to the manifest behavior, thoughts, and feelings that are causing the trouble in the person's life adjustment. The assumption is that it is easier for people to change if they discover why they are the way they are; that is, if they discover the irrational within themselves. However, I also believe people can change without realizing what internal changes are accompanying the external and obvious changes. Man was maturing before psychiatrists existed; he did so because life demanded he do so.

Young people have a remarkable capacity for change; this book should, therefore, be most helpful to the young. Although they are usually pliable and changeable, their belief that there is always time later on for changing sometimes becomes a powerful resistance to changing. Some older people can achieve extensive change with very little help under the pressure of realizing the high cost in personal suffering, and the psychological damage to their children, if they do not change. Another great inducer of change for some older people who are not too ill is the realization that they are running out of time; it is a matter of now or never.

There is a natural tendency in everyone not to change. The element of the unknown contributes to this; however, the primary reason relates to the presence of unconscious forces within the personality. If there were not a barrier of resistance in the mind, the contents of the unconscious would become conscious. Behaving in a more mature way tends to force unconscious conflicts into the conscious; for many, this is frightening. Furthermore, habitual ways of behaving acquire a rigidity which resist change. Anxiety, depression, or both, and at times psychiatric syndromes, may appear as individuals change. More mature behavior requires the individual to stand alone, and to do so awakens repressed separation anxiety. Mature behavior also requires the individual to be responsible, involved, and more masterful. These shifts awaken unconscious conflicts having to do with threats and guilt which prevented the person from behaving more maturely in the first place.

Another basis for resistance to change, and one which usually leads to some degree of depression during the course of change, has to do with the internal losses within the unconscious mind. For instance, a woman who is succeeding in her efforts to become more feminine will frequently become depressed as she gives up her unconscious attachment to her father with whom she had identified. Changing also requires the individual to give up his old way of life including, on occasion, certain ongoing environmental attachments—further cause for depression.

It is imperative that those who embark on a serious effort to improve their lives should proceed at a rate which does not bring on too severe anxiety, depression, or some form of psychic disorganization. Conversely, the various signs of psychic distress should not be feared if the person experiencing them can continue to function reasonably well. In a married couple various signs of distress are often used by one party as a means by which to intimidate the other and to cause a reduction in pressure for change. Change never comes easily; nor is it ever steady. There are times when it may seem that the project is hopeless. It is at these times *in particular* that one must remain committed to his goals and *persist*.

Guiding Principles for Making Family Life Successful

The most important task facing a man and woman who marry is to evoke the best qualities in one another—for the man to fully awaken the woman in his

wife and for the woman to fully awaken the man in her
husband. When this happens, the likelihood of a deeply
loving and committed relationship is great. The stage is
then set for children to be reared properly. Once a family is formed it is vital that the man and woman relate
to each other and to their children in a way which provides the best possible climate for the children. This
means that a certain organizational pattern must be
established within the family, with the man as head of
the family and a clear division of the responsibilities for
the father and mother, especially in relation to the children.

Those who have not achieved what is possible in
marriage, and who elect to follow the guidelines previously set forth, can expect turbulence in their lives until
they have sustained a new level of adjustment for some
length of time, thereby giving maturational processes
time to take place and become firmly established. It may
take several months, or a year, or more, to achieve the
desired goal. Persistent and committed effort is the key
to success.

The *first principle* is for both the man and woman to
realize there are two parts to the personalities of each, a
healthy or mature part and an unhealthy or sick part. A
strong bond must be established between the healthy
parts of the husband and wife, and the sick parts in
each must be seen as something to be disposed of. When
the disagreeable aspect of the other's personality is seen
as "sick" there is no reason to be angry at the other
person. The following vignette illustrates this principle.

A very aggressive female patient said to me that she
could see that I didn't like grouchiness in women. I said
she was correct. "Then you don't like me," was her response. I said she was wrong. I liked the woman in her
that showed through periodically, but that I did not like
her grouchiness. I continued by saying that it was a
good thing I didn't like it, because if I did, it would be
unlikely that I could change her. I added that I did not
like illness in any form and I considered her grouchiness
to be a symptom of her illness.

The *second principle* requires the male to first look at himself and identify where and how he is not living up to the values which define the conduct of the head of the family. In conjunction with his self-inspection he should ask his wife to point out his shortcomings. He should start the process by first changing himself. As he changes he must then expect the same of his wife and point out her shortcomings. She, too, must be willing to look at herself. The point to be grasped is that the primary responsibility for initiating change and insuring that change continues *rests with the man*. Nonetheless, both should follow the guidelines spelled out throughout this book. There is no reason for the woman to wait for her husband to initiate the process of change. It works best when both parties participate wholeheartedly; however, the ultimate responsibility rests on the shoulders of the man; if he starts to change, many women (and children) will too.

The *third principle* is that criticism must be abandoned. Criticism only evokes resentment and frequently fear; it rarely brings out the best in the person being criticized. Noting someone's faults can be done in a way that is not critical. Nagging at someone is destructive, never constructive.

The *fourth principle* pertains to the expression of anger, which inevitably is evoked as both parties expect the other to change. I have rarely seen expressions of anger accomplish anything constructive except in very special instances. No one can go through life without expressing anger toward even those he loves the most; however, regularly giving vent to one's anger and criticalness toward one's spouse usually makes matters worse, especially during the process of changing the personalities of a married couple and their marital patterns. When anger is felt it can and should be expressed in any of a number of ways, but in private. Some find it useful to swear, others to engage in physical activity; it should not be directed toward the spouse. This is a very difficult principle to live by, especially when the spouse has done something provocative or destructive. At such times the behavior should be pointed out and appropriate action taken, but the associated anger should be expressed privately. To direct anger at one's spouse usually amounts to taking the other's bait, that is, reacting to the spouse's behavior in order to satisfy his or her unconscious need to create distance and disharmony and even to destroy the relationship. Remember, it is in the nature of things for male and female to live together harmoniously according to certain patterns.

The *fifth principle* requires the spouse to acknowledge and reward mature behavior in the other. Everyone needs praise and positive reinforcement for new achievements. Learning theorists make much of this, and I believe they are right. Children learn more rapidly and cheerfully if they receive rewards each time they take a step forward. The same applies to adults. Progress should be sincerely rewarded. How this is done is a matter for the couple involved to work out. Simple recognition and expressions of appreciation go a long way.

The *sixth principle* has to do with providing the ability to change. For an old way of behaving to be abandoned and a new way achieved, the strength and courage to do so must come from somewhere. Patients in psychiatric treatment receive this, in part, from their doctor. A good doctor will help point the way; he will remove the unconscious barriers blocking progress, or at least make them known, and if necessary he will provide the encouragement necessary for the patient to change. Persons not in treatment can find the strength to change from encouragement given by their spouse, and by drawing upon their own willpower.

The *seventh principle* pertains to the use of force. Force in itself is not evil or destructive. The purpose for which force is used defines its value. Force can be applied in a variety of ways. A woman can force her husband to behave more maturely by refusing to assume his responsibilities. Similarly, a man can refuse to do his wife's work and thereby force her to do it. There is another application of force which falls to the one primarily responsible for the integrity and survival of the fam-

ily—the man. When observation, discussion, encouragement, support, and persuasion by the man fail to bring
about the desired changes in his wife, he must apply
force. He can prevent (force) his wife from doing certain
things and by using one kind of leverage or another he
must insist she begin doing that which she is not doing.
It is remarkable how many good things begin to happen
when the man simply "lays down the law." I have never
known a woman to fail to admit (in private) that this is
precisely what she wanted her husband to do, when she
was getting away with destructive or irresponsible ways
of behaving with her husband or her family, or in general. Male and female are biologically different. It is the
male's superior strength and greater aggressiveness
which places the final responsibility on him for changing
his own and his wife's behavior. If it takes the application of force to fulfill his responsibilities, then he must
use it—wisely and in properly measured doses, but use
it he must.

Couples face a difficult problem when the man cannot assume this responsibility. What final leverage does
the wife have when the application of the preceding principles fail, particularly the use of encouragement? It may
be necessary for her to threaten to divorce her husband
if he does not change for the better. This threat may be
viewed as the *eighth principle*. Such a threat often ini-
tiates the process of change, making it possible for the
couple to then apply the other seven principles. The
man also may threaten to divorce his wife if all else
fails.

There is a serious drawback to threats of divorce,
however. If the couple is sufficiently disturbed such
threats play into the illness of both and may actually
facilitate the destruction of the marriage rather than
initiate a process of constructive change. The threat of
divorce should only be used as a last resort and never as
an anger-provoking threat or as a means by which to
manipulate and intimidate the other party and thereby
attain a selfish goal. Further, it is an admission of defeat, a fact which neither party may be willing to accept.

When the use of these principles fails to bring about change, psychiatric assistance should be sought. When such help is unavailable or proves to be ineffective, the couple will have to decide whether to remain married or to divorce.

Values and Guidelines

The values and patterns of living which lead to harmony in a childless couple may be somewhat different from those which should govern the living patterns of a married couple with children. For instance, the consequences are less serious if the woman is aggressive and domineering and the man passive. It is unlikely that either party would be truly happy and fulfilled, but if they think they are, and are free from psychiatric symptoms and can remain so, what difference does it make? Sooner or later, though, such couples usually show signs of discontent or more serious strain.

However, when children arrive, it is very important that the man and woman establish certain definite patterns within their family and find harmony too. It cannot be repeated too many times that for children to grow into mature men and women their father must have been a masculine man, their mother a feminine woman, and a harmonious relationship must have existed between them. However, this harmony must be consistent with the model of the ideal family.

The top executive of an organization should be kind, willing to listen, firm when necessary but not harsh or unreasonable. There should be no question that the final authority and responsibility rest with him. A good executive endeavors to bring out the very best in each person in his organization and to promote individual and organizational growth.

There is nothing about these formulations which should suggest that the woman should be seen but not heard, or that femininity is weak and second-rate. A mature woman is a substantial person, capable of many things in life. Through her intellect, wisdom, and awareness of the most meaningful factors affecting the members of her family, she will contribute greatly to the direction the lives of all will take. But so will the man; and the final responsibility and authority must rest with him. It is he who is most at the interface between society at large and his family. He is the primary and ultimate protector of the family.

Improving a Marriage

Many married couples eat and sleep together, have children, but rarely speak to each other; they never just sit and talk, and, worse, they rarely spend time alone with each other. Having acknowledged this mutual problem, they must make the effort to talk on topics of mutual interest. Incredible events may begin to occur. Anxiety will almost surely arise in both; irritabilities will be expressed; avoidant devices will be used; excuses and tricks of one kind or another will be employed so as to avoid the effort to increase the involvement with the spouse. These tricks must be rigorously searched out and thwarted. With continued effort this pattern will change and a new measure of intimacy will have been achieved.

Talking leads to loving and to mutual respect. Broadly based cooperativeness is the ultimate objective. I do not wish to imply that just by talking with each other couples can achieve an idyllic marriage—by no means—but talking is an important place to start.

The most frequent complaint I have heard from women about their husbands is that they can push their husbands around. They are equally resentful of their husband's refusal (or inability) to participate in family life. They complain that they remain too aloof from the family, that they are irresponsible with money, that they fail to be an authority and establish guidelines for the family, and for the children in particular. They especially deplore the fact that the husbands pay little attention to the children. In short, these women have to assume many of the responsibilities which should fall to the man; men like these—the passive, weak, and/or remote—force the woman into the male's role. The wives of such men have to become father and mother. Some of these men may be quite masterful at work but completely and passively dominated by their wives at home. The women end up doing most of what the men should do; they complain about it, and yet they may complain even more if the man starts to take his rightful place within the family.

Since it is sometimes easier for others to make observations about an individual than for the individual to be able to observe himself, it is vital that the woman communicate her observations about her husband to him when they begin to talk more to each other. No matter how difficult the challenge may seem to her, despite hesitation, anxiety, and especially in the face of her inner tendency to maintain the status quo, the wife should communicate her observations to her husband, and in as kind and gentle a manner as is possible encourage him to change. She should never do this in a hostile or nagging way, for to do so will only reinforce his own internal "critics"—those deposits of the past which have stood in the way of his complete maturation. His anxiety and self-doubt will be unduly increased by his wife's attack and the attack from within himself. His early, and often halting, efforts to change should be rewarded by encouragement and praise. These should be communicated in such a way that the man is never made to feel like a "little boy who is doing better," but as a man who is burdened by an illness which he is progressively overcoming. The attitude in both should be, "We are working and gaining on *it*"—"it" being the illness which is not his fault but the changing of which is now being striven for. A very useful view is to look upon these troublesome traits, behaviors, and attitudes as foreign bodies, things which are really not an integral part of the essential man.

The point to be grasped is that when a partially (psychologically) crippled man begins to achieve his proper identity and take his rightful place in the family, the wife must respond to this in a womanly way. He should take charge of the finances, sit at the head of the table, attend to the repair needs of the home, pay the bills, take responsibility for the investment program,

spend more time with the family, etc.; all with her cooperation.

A man who is beginning to find his manliness will
quickly observe behaviors in his wife which are aggressive, bossy, and avoidant of certain responsibilities, and
so on. It now falls to him as the head of the home to see
to it that she fulfills her role. Holding the woman to her
responsibilities, and preventing her from behaving in
her old ways, can be done firmly and kindly. Unless the
woman is extremely ill emotionally she will respond positively to her husband if the stakes are high and she has
made the commitment to make a success of their relationship. The stakes are always high when there are
children still in the home, and even when they have left.

He will give her courage to blossom as a woman, but
he may have to do more than that too. A formidable
challenge for him will be to stand in the way of those
behaviors in his wife which derive from her envy of the
male, her identification with her father, and identification with a somewhat unfeminine mother. If she cannot
change her ways through her own efforts and through
his encouragement and support, the sparks may quite
literally begin to fly as he begins to apply force and at
the same time prevent her from "running home to
mother"—or to her attorney.

As the husband insists that his wife relinquish her
dominant position in the family, she will probably resent having to make these changes. These are crucial
and deciding moments which may take on crisis proportions, and the fate of the family depends on their outcome. Sometimes a woman refuses to change and threatens to leave the husband if he persists in his demands
on her and in his pursuit of his rightful place in the
family. This threat on her part is actually self-protective
in its meaning, for the prospect of changing can create
extreme anxiety. These are women who have very little
of a loving and security-giving mother inside them. They
may have internalized a harsh and rejecting "bad" mother
also. Furthermore, these women seem to know intuitively
that the threat of being left is a vulnerability of their

husbands; that is, the threat of being left by the wife
awakens the old unconscious fear of being left by the
mother. The mothers of weak men often disciplined their
sons by threatening (by words or attitude) to leave or
abandon them if they didn't obey.

The man must stand firm and not be intimidated by
his wife's threat to leave. He is now receiving his su-
preme test; if he yields his position the illness in his wife
and in himself will have won. The spirit of cooperativeness may be lost temporarily, but the man must stand
firm. While some women do leave as they threaten to do,
most merely make the threat while secretly hoping the
man will stand firm, and not let her continue to dominate and get away with her aggressive, bossy ways. To
be left as a child is disastrous, and to have this fear
awakened by an angry, threatening wife has caused many
men to back down when they should have stood firm.

The nearly inevitable result when the man holds his
ground is that the woman will begin to cooperate and
give up her domineering ways—often to the complete
surprise of the man and frequently to the woman as
well. Standing firm on the man's part, without fear, is
the key to success of many relationships where it has
been the woman's pattern to dominate and run roughshod
over the man. Many women have the wish to deprive the
man of his maleness, to diminish and dominate him—
castrate him. When the man demonstrates by his behavior that this cannot be done, the air is cleared and the
stage set for a more cooperative and rewarding relationship. This then makes it possible for family life to proceed in a way which will insure the proper development
of children and the greatest happiness for the man and
woman.

The woman's domination may take a great many
forms. She may control the money; have her way in most
or all family decisions, minor or major; be the primary
authority with the children; be the aggressor in sexual
relations; influence his career (positively if she wishes to
be the power behind the scene and negatively if she is
determined to destroy the male); openly or subtly de-

mean him; and in severe cases, behave in ways which promote disintegration in him.

Some of the signs of the woman's rejection of her feminine role and the underlying conflicts leading to this rejection, in addition to those which have already been mentioned, include: sexual or general frigidity; a messy home, including haphazard care of her own personal belongings, particularly underclothing; an unwillingness to socialize, particularly with the families of her husband's business or professional associates; absence of women friends; the belief that work in the home is demeaning to her; inability to cooperate in the spending of money; overspending for trivial and nonessential items; the need to acquire possessions of limited usefulness; many more clothes, especially shoes, than necessary; resentment of her husband's financial planning on the grounds that she and the family are being deprived (this may include resentment of his insurance planning for *her* security); chronic dissatisfaction about anything and everything.

Many of the woman's destructive ways and anti-feminine personality traits will come to light, as a couple who have made the commitment to improve their marriage begin to work on the task of changing. If basic change is to be the result, then the man must not permit the preceding kinds of behaviors to continue in his wife and she, in turn, must communicate her anxiety, depression, resentment, etc., to her husband *and not pull away from him*. He is her best ally, not her enemy. To pull away would only increase the distance between them. Less basic change will occur, or her behavior may change slightly, but the couple will be living at arm's length with neither finding much gratification from the other. Instead, the wife must turn to her husband and obtain comfort and courage from him and praise for having changed. It is crucial that the man who is inducing change in his wife stand by her as she changes. She has the right to expect him to stand by her, and it is his responsibility not to let her down. The project may well be scuttled by his failure to be ready to respond in a security-giving, comforting, and also masculine way to his newly changed, or changing, wife. Many men want their wives to change, to be more feminine, but when they change the husbands find they are not up to responding to the changed wife.

Both parties must continually remind themselves of their commitment and not lose sight of their goal. They must turn to each other for comfort and security until such time as they have increased their courage and have become more self-confident. Setbacks will be inevitable, but a good marital relationship wherein both live out their roles in ways consonant with nature's endowments is entirely possible if both cooperate and persist.

The application of force when other inducements for change have failed is one of the most loving things a man can do for his wife. He is, in effect, insisting that she give up her illness and achieve health. When a woman's resistance to change is extreme, the use of sudden expressions of anger and iron-like firmness may be necessary and are usually quite effective. It is best to rely on firmness alone if at all possible. Firmness must be followed up by love, support, and praise. These human qualities which the woman receives from her husband will quiet the anxiety which the process of change will have generated within her.

The following headings refer to a number of common battlegrounds upon which married couples reveal the presence of irrational forces within themselves. My objective in discussing these special situations is to spell out some of the unconscious meanings.

Money

With regard to money, there usually is just so much to go around, and ideally the husband and wife will cooperatively plan their finances. When, however, the wife refuses to cooperate the husband must take complete charge. It is quite likely that a more rational allocation of money can be arrived at if both work cooperatively on the task, but where the wife refuses she must be forced or matters must be taken out of her hands. In time, if she can commit herself to the goal of a good marriage—and both must continually remind themselves of their common goal—she will change. It is remarkable how much money can be saved when the wife cooperates with a responsible husband. Her inability to cooperate is clearly an attempt to defeat her husband, to rob him of his power. He who controls the money has the power.

Unfortunately, many men are irresponsible with family finances and they force their wives to take this responsibility against their own wish to do so. The woman often protests having to take the financial responsibility, and many women would gladly turn over the management of finances to their husbands if they would, or could, assume this responsibility. When men squander money on nonessentials, fail to plan for the future, for emergencies, etc., the wife is left no choice but to take control of the money, and usually of other areas of family life as well.

Some of the fiercest marital battles are fought over money. It is in this arena that the spirit of cooperativeness toward the objective of making a real marriage is most likely to be lost. The control of money provides one of the best means for a symptomatic expression of the unconscious wish for power. By far the most common way the woman betrays her competitiveness toward the male, and her inability to enter into a cooperative heterosexual relationship, is by spending money foolishly. This is done by buying nonessentials, paying top prices instead of looking for bargains, buying too many bargains, and so on.

A mature married couple will have no difficulty whatsoever with their finances. Both will have full knowledge of their financial situation, and both will cooperate in the spending of money. In the absence of unconscious meanings attached to money, married couples will be able to allocate their funds in accordance with the immediate and long-range needs of their family. Some women have excellent money sense. Men with wives like this are fools if they reject their wife's counsel.

Fidelity and Sex

Statistics show that the divorce rate is higher in couples who have lived together before marriage than in those who court each other and then marry. Living together does not reflect freedom from psychological and sexual conflicts—just the opposite in most instances. Living together implies difficulty with loving and sexual commitment. This deficit is ultimately reflected in the higher divorce rate. That is to say, when the couple who have been living together finally marry in the formal sense, something happens to upset an equilibrium. The greater degree of commitment triggers unconscious conflicts that had lain relatively dormant. Having been triggered, they produce internal discomfort (anxiety, guilt, etc.). "Incompatibility" then begins to appear between the couple, creating distance between them. This distance in turn reduces the conflict each is having on the other, and their own unconscious conflicts sink into the deeper regions of the mind. Less inner discomfort is felt by both parties, even though they may experience some distress about the distance between them.

The idea of being faithful to your spouse is considered by many to be old-fashioned and puritanical. An increasing number of self-proclaimed authorities, some of whom are professionals and many of whom are not, are propagandizing the public with claims that monogamy is dead. They advocate "swinging," loose "marital" relationships, marriage by contract, group living, mate-swapping, etc. Some even claim that infidelity is a growth-producing experience. All of this is very bad advice and destructive in its effect on the individual, the marriage, and above all on the family. None of this advice is based on solid evidence which show that such ways of life are constructive in either the short or long run.

A mature couple who have a good marriage will have no need whatsoever for any of the above experiences and, in particular, for clandestine infidelity. A couple embarked on a project of self-help, or a couple receiving psychotherapeutic help, should never be unfaithful. The objective is to resolve unconscious conflicts and alter their behavioral consequences so that a fully committed heterosexual relationship becomes possible.

Infidelity is usually caused by the inability to express both love and sexual feelings toward the same person. The most common reason for this behavior is the failure to have overcome childhood guilt about erotic feelings towards the parent of the opposite sex. For the unfaithful man, his wife will usually represent the respected, admired mother while the mistress will be the representation of the mother of his boyhood days for whom he had strong sexual feelings. These repressed memories and associated guilt prevent the man from both loving and experiencing a full measure of sexual pleasure with his wife. The same formulation applies to the woman. She projects her unconscious wishes onto her husband; that is, she has a transference reaction toward him and does not experience him as just the man she married. Frustrated and unsatisfied because of her inability to find romantic and sexual gratification with him, she may turn to a lover.

Couples burdened by the unconscious conflicts I have just described may be cooperative in their sexual relations but because they cannot find pleasure they look elsewhere. Some couples find pleasure with each other but are unfaithful anyway. The usual pattern, however, is the one where the couple is desirous of sexual pleasure with each other, but manage to provoke arguments or hard feelings so that the sexual encounter does not occur or, if it does, proves to be unsatisfactory. This is seen most frequently in women. The husband makes known his interest in having sexual relations and the wife manages to do something which provokes anger in him. Her maneuver may be extremely subtle, such as an attitude of slightly bored tolerance of the act, or she may bring up some unrelated issue and provoke her husband, or she may simply be cold and rejecting. One of the most common patterns of all is that in which the couple has spent a pleasurable day together, the logical and wished for (by both) conclusion of which would be sexual intercourse. As the time approaches for lovemaking to occur, one or both will provoke the other into an argument or become obviously uninterested, using an evasive maneuver.

When these evasions and provocations occur frequently, they provide one or both parties a ready excuse for looking elsewhere for sexual pleasure. While provocative and rejecting behavior is a secondary basis for infidelity, it is not its true basis. Provocations, rejection, and the like are the means to the end, the end being the destruction of loving and sexual intimacy.

It is remarkable how married individuals will sometimes temporarily experience greater sexual pleasure with a lover. The lover may or may not be more expert than the spouse, frequently even less so, and is often much less admirable or possessive of strength of character and other fine qualities. It is the uncommitted aspect of the illicit relationship which makes greater pleasure possible. Unconscious conflicts are not so fully mobilized in the unfaithful person as when attempting to relate to the spouse to whom he is committed. This principle can be clearly illustrated by the following apparently curious phenomenon. Some married couples can feel love for each other and experience sexual delight before marriage but after the marriage vows have been made sexual difficulties (frigidity or impotence) appear. Some couples grow distant except for sexual pleasure. Sexual relations may become the only time the two are ever together in any way. They can have sex but not closeness. Some couples have closeness but little sex.

In order for a couple to overcome the barrier between them and finally resolve these unconscious conflicts, they must not cheat on each other but must, instead, try very hard to break down the barrier and experience a full range of feeling (love and sex) for each other. I think it is unwise for couples to confess their infidelities to each other; much hurt may result which may never be overcome.

As a man becomes more assertive in his relationship with his wife he may find he will be temporarily disturbed in his capacity to perform sexually. The unconscious conflicts which have been mobilized by his becoming more manly with his wife are the true bases for his impaired sexual functioning. It is of the greatest importance that the wife not react to these setbacks in functioning in a hostile fashion. Instead, she must be understanding, tolerant, and helpful. She must, above all, give her man time to change and overcome his anxiety and sexual dysfunction, just as he must for her.

In a relationship where sex has little meaning, both parties should work at achieving a richer sex life if they want to get the most out of their marriage. Here some of the most difficult resistances to change may be encountered. A domineering, aggressive woman who has never overcome her penis envy, oedipal attachments, and other unconscious conflicts may experience much difficulty in behaving in a responsive, receptive manner which evokes the best from her man. It will be difficult for her to eliminate the competitive quality in her sexual behavior, or her impatience, her disgust, or her need to demean her husband. These behaviors and attitudes are all designed to prevent the woman in her from coming out, and also prevent the occurrence of an intimate experience with her husband during which both cooperate and respond to each other. A feminine woman is not an unresponsive, passive mass during lovemaking. She is receptive and responsive.

The couple embarked on a program of self-help (and those in treatment too) should not be embarrassed to talk about their anxiety and misgivings associated with the sex act. They should try to help each other overcome inhibitions and discard ways of behaving which deviate from mature sexual behavior. First to be achieved is the recognition in both parties that trouble exists, and next to be achieved is an attitude of frank, wholehearted cooperativeness.

A married couple should be able to share the plea-

sure of sex freely and cooperatively. Ideally this should
be achieved by sexual intercourse. A couple who attempt
to improve their marriage should strive for the highest
goals, sexual pleasure being only one among many, but
they should not be disheartened and believe their marriage to be a failure if they are unable to reach this
particular goal. There are a multitude of facets to a good
marriage. Sexual pleasure is only one of them. Sex tends
to fall into place if the rest of the marriage is satisfying.
I am quite certain that a mature married couple will
find no need for infidelity.

Children as a Maturational Stimulus

A powerful stimulus to the maturational processes
in a married couple is the coming of children. I do not
recommend having a child for "therapeutic" purposes;
however, when children do appear it is imperative that
the parents behave in ways which favor the best possible maturation for the child as well as for themselves.

Some women who are still burdened by separation
anxiety and penis envy, and who did not receive adequate mothering, will treat their infant as if it were an
object to be used for the purpose of abating their loneliness and quieting their anxiety; it makes up for what is
"missing." They are inclined to view the child as a part
of their own body. The child becomes the penis they
have long awaited, or it may serve as a kind of "security
blanket." This unrealistic view of the child leads to behaviors which are severely detrimental to the child's
development and contributes to the breakdown of the
marriage. Such a mother will devote excessive time and
energy to her child; she now feels complete and has little
need for her husband. The husband will generally withdraw angrily; he may find a mistress, spew hostility
onto his wife and child, and so forth. The intensity of his
reaction will depend to a large extent on the degree to
which he is unconsciously burdened.

A young mother should nurse her child, and this is
an experience she should enjoy; it will be one which will
stimulate the maturational process within her. The fa-

ther of the child should be able to take pride in his wife
and view the nursing mother with fondness and not
jealousy and envy. He will be able to do this when he
has stored in him the good experiences with his own
mother. In short, unless there is a physiological limita-
tion in the mother, she should try her best to nurse her
child and continue to do so until it is ready to stop
nursing.

I do not think it best for young mothers to work and
relegate their infant's care to others. Some men resent
their wives staying at home with their child. This attitude should be overcome and pride taken in the wife
who wants to make a home. She will more likely find
contentment in this task if she is given the rewards of a
loving and appreciative husband.

It is very common for couples who have been happy
together to draw apart after the coming of a child. This
fact can be accounted for by the mobilization of unconscious conflicts in addition to those just mentioned. With
the coming of a child, a triangle—a family—has been
created. This situation serves as a powerful trigger of
unconscious oedipal conflicts formed in the couple's own
childhoods. It is as if the young wife is experiencing
herself in her mother's place with her father, and the
husband his own father's place with the mother. In order to allow these unconscious conflicts to recede, both
parties will tend to move away from each other. Both
become unhappy and restless, and divorce may ensue.

The new child will also serve as a powerful maturational stimulus causing a crystallization of gender identity and sex role responsibility for both the father and
mother. The wife, who may have worked, will now have
to stay at home and attend to her maternal responsibilities and opportunities. More responsibilities will fall to
the man. All of these changes, along with the new conflict-triggering family constellation, may produce frank
psychiatric symptoms, anxiety, depression in one or both,
and almost surely will cause the couple to draw apart if
they are burdened by unconscious conflicts, and closer
together if they are mature.

In keeping with their original goal and commitment, the couple who wish to help themselves will strive to make a family in the best sense of the word. The new family will sharpen their perception of the nature of their relationship and facilitate the identification of abnormal attitudes, feelings, and behaviors.

When the man sees his wife rejecting her child, he should not take over her role unless the wife is extremely hard pressed. He should, instead, try to support and encourage her. It is remarkable how much more effective women can be in the home if they receive encouragement from their husbands. Similarly, when the husband avoids his children, the wife should point this out to him. Each should encourage the other to live up to his responsibilities as mother and father in such a way as to provide the family patterns of healthy development for their children.

Parents are, of course, absolutely essential for children. Children do a great deal for their parents. Not only do they provide joys which can be found nowhere else, but they can bring out the very best in men and women. Men who are successful as fathers will usually be successful in their life's work. Not all men who are successful at their work are successful family men. This simply points out that a special kind of maturity is necessary for a man to be a successful father.

Many women who are quite successful in a career are total failures as mothers. The emotional involvements and responsibilities of motherhood trigger their unconscious conflicts and they become ill and/or fail.

Other Problems
Demanding Maturation

Establishing a Heterosexual Relationship
Unmarried people are in the position of having to pull themselves up by their own bootstraps. There are, however, social forces as well as those internal ones which propel persons toward maturity. The unmarried

person does not, however, have the spouse as a source of courage, observation, and as a conflict trigger; all factors which will stimulate maturation.

A young person who avoids the opposite sex is almost certainly burdened by unconscious conflicts. Given freedom from unconscious conflicts and a social situation where opportunities exist, males and females will come together; Nature is at work.

Unmarried persons frequently complain about insufficient opportunities for meeting a suitable person. These are mostly rationalizations; the persons in question are denying the effects of their own behavior which drive persons of the opposite sex away and can in this way justify avoiding the opposite sex. There are life situations where the opposite sex is absent or where it might be prudent to avoid such contacts; but, given the usual life circumstances, the man or woman who avoids forming a relationship with the opposite sex usually has something wrong with him or her.

These remarks are not to be understood as advocating that everyone *must* form a heterosexual commitment because of the severity of their personality disturbances. A child might accidentally be born (at the worst), and/or an overt mental disturbance might erupt if they attempted to form a heterosexual relationship.

It could be argued that those persons who are inhibited in relation to the opposite sex should be left alone and not urged to overcome their difficulties; the chances are fairly high that they will overcome them. The chances are fairly high they will make a bad marriage and produce children who will develop some form of personality disturbance. There is much merit to this argument; however, even persons with marked personality disturbances seek out the opposite sex, they do marry, and children are born. The forces of nature which bring male and female together are very powerful. It is better, therefore, to help them become as emotionally healthy as possible for the sake of the children they may have. Everyone has the right to be as healthy as it is possible to be. Finally, those who can find satisfaction in a heterosexual relationship are usually happier than persons who live more isolated lives.

A good place for a young man to start is to turn to his own father or, when this is impossible, to a teacher, coach, friend, or any older man who has himself achieved a successful marriage—and has also reared healthy children. This may be very difficult for an inhibited young man to do. He may think he senses disapproval from the other man. He may have a transference reaction (project repressed feelings toward his own father onto other men) to all or most older men; if not, he may soon develop such a reaction when his intentions to establish a relationship with a female become the reason for his association with the older man.

Immense good can be done by parents or parental figures for young persons. In fact, more good may be achieved than from certain professionals. Frankly, I would be inclined to rely more on the impact of a good, strong, mature man or woman on a troubled young person than on many of the professionals I have known.

The young man should speak frankly of his fears, misgivings, uncertainties, and guard against a sense of having weakened or diminished himself by having asked for advice, guidance, and encouragement. He and this father, or father substitute, should meet periodically to discuss his progress or lack thereof. He should point out the ways the younger man is failing or stacking the cards against himself. He should guide, advise, and encourage. Once the younger man has sought out the older man, the latter should see to it that their relationship endures. The stronger must take responsibility for the weaker. Parents must remember that they never cease being parents.

The major difficulty with these guidelines is that the younger man may turn to someone who is psychiatrically troubled himself and who ascribes to a value system which is largely a function of his own unconscious conflicts. I am referring to hypermorality manifested by an excessively strict code of behavior or, conversely, a psychiatrically disturbed man who advocates various forms of immature behavior to a younger man. Therefore, I repeat, the person to whom the younger one turns for help should be a *man* in the best sense of the word, and one who ascribes to the values referred to throughout this book. A happily married man with children, who is the head of his family, who is successful in his work, is the kind of man to use as a helper. You will be surprised to find so many people who are willing to help if they are asked; this includes one's own parents.

Unfortunately, the severely troubled young man who needs help to make a successful heterosexual adjustment may not have the kind of father who can provide the kind of assistance he needs. The worst that can happen to a young man who turns to his father is to be confronted by a father who is competitive with him, or who hates and rejects him. Such fathers can give a young man, even their son, very bad advice. Had the father been a better father the son probably would not have become psychiatrically troubled in the first place. This point requires some elaboration, however.

Many times circumstances have taken the father away when the young boy needed him; military service or vocational duties, for instance. The father may have been very neurotic himself and his marriage not a good one when the son was a child. Life events may have matured the father in the meantime. Thus, years later, after having matured, eventually having made a good marriage, etc., he might now be suitable as someone to guide his teen–age or adult son in his efforts to establish a heterosexual relationship.

The key to success in such situations is for the helper to feel his responsibilities for the successful adjustment of the younger man and do whatever his wisdom and judgment point to as needing to be done. A parent is never free from all responsibility to his children. The person giving help may need to ask the young one about very specific details in his efforts with women, tell him to refrain from some actions, initiate others, and so on. The psychic significance of this enterprise is that the younger man looks to the "good father" for help. With the mother no longer the object of the son's intentions, as was the situation when the young man was a boy of three to six, success is likely to ensue. There is no longer a basis for rivalry, competition, fear, or hate except in the unconscious mind of the younger man. If the older man sees evidence of a negative reaction in the young one to the advice he is giving, he should not take this personally but realize that the younger man is reacting inappropriately on the basis of feelings which are stored in his unconscious mind. The father or father figure will be helping the young man give up his unconscious attachment to his mother and find a girl of his own. This unconscious process will be taking place silently in the young man as he makes a successful heterosexual relationship.

What has been outlined for the young man who is having difficulty associating with the opposite sex, or who cannot make a commitment to a woman, applies equally to a young woman. She should turn to an older and mature woman for help, preferably one who has married and had children. Her mother may or may not be suitable; if suitable from the standpoint of her own maturity, she is the most desirable one to turn to.

Young people frequently have difficulty talking to their parents. If they can communicate with their parents, the word of the parent generally carries more weight than that of others. Young people will usually be very surprised by how easy it is for them to talk to their parents once the parents are given a chance to help. The young person may eventually have to turn to several older persons and accept the best each has to give. *Don't give up!*

The chance for a successful outcome is increased if there is frank talk about all aspects of male-female interactions. Silent processes of change will be taking place which are vital to the young person's maturity. First, factual information will have to be obtained; next, the young person will have to master new situations. Crippling unconscious conflicts will be mobilized by the new behavior, making it possible for the healthy parts of his personality to resolve them; and finally, an identification process with an older person of the same sex will be taking place. This combination of a close working relationship with an older (and mature) person, while simultaneously making efforts to establish a relationship with and commitment to a person of the opposite sex of one's own age is one of the most maturing life situations. The young person and the older person who are working together cannot strive for insight deep into the unconscious; they are not trained for this task. Helping the younger one discover the most successful and mature ways for behaving generally and with the opposite sex in particular is the objective. Such a relationship makes up to some extent for the good fathering (in the male) and good mothering (in the female) the young person missed out on as a child. Such supportive relationships are extremely helpful and can markedly alter the course of a young person's life and may even be lifesaving if properly handled.

Nothing of what I have just said about the importance of making a heterosexual relationship should be understood to mean that I advocate early marriage. Fifty percent of early marriages end in divorce. This is not surprising. Young people often marry for the wrong reasons. They use marriage as a means to combat loneliness, to provide an easy and ready accessibility for sexual gratification. They are driven into marriage by unconscious forces. Young people should associate with a number of different persons of the opposite sex, thereby giving themselves time to mature, before making a final commitment.

What determines the choice of a mate is a complex subject. One element in the choice of a mate is crucial and must not be ignored. This has to do with masculinity in men and femininity in women. When a young man makes the decision to marry, he should be mature enough to pick a woman who is not bossy, domineering, and aggressive, or ineffectual in her efforts to be a woman.

Even when young people do not seek help from older persons or from their parents, I firmly believe parents should keep close watch on the dating patterns of their sons and daughters. When parents see their daughters pick weak, ineffectual, or effeminate boys or men, or their sons date aggressive, domineering women, and especially if they date masculinized women, they should intervene. This can be done tactfully but in a way which may lead to a reassessment of the relationship and its consequences if a marriage were to be entered into.

Parents Must Look at Themselves

For parents to be able to make such an intervention in their son's or daughter's personal life, it will require them to first look at themselves and see what it was about their relationship with each other and their child which caused him to be the kind of person he is. These can be extremely hard facts to face, but face them you must if you do not wish to perpetuate a tradition of disturbed marital relationships and disturbed personalities in your family tree.

I urge parents and their son or daughter to read this book and discuss it, and then to look into their past history of their lives together. It may be possible for sons to finally work out a better relationship with their fathers and mature in the process (the father may mature too). Similarly, mothers and daughters may at long last fully find each other. This will not be an easy task; many will fail, but those parents and offspring whose personalities are not too disturbed will succeed.

Parents are their children's keepers. Never forget it. Correct the mistakes which your own personalities and your not completely successful marriage forced you to make with your children. Intervene with your children (even though they are young adults) and do it effectively. There is no greater good to be done for them or for mankind than preventing your children from making bad marriages.

Becoming Successful at Work

Another aspect of maturity is the capacity to work effectively, productively, and with a sense of joy. Many people find their way into a life's work which suits them, that is, which permits the expression of their primary interests, talents, or skills, but who—because of conflicts within themselves—cannot fully realize their potential. They are not ill suited for their vocation or profession but unconscious forces prevent their becoming successful. Such persons are blocked by unconscious conflicts and these usually involve insecurity and/or guilt about being successful, or both.

The first step toward self-help with regard to one's work is the recognition that one is not achieving his potentials fully, either through avoidant behavior (missing opportunities for advancement), or by provoking rejection by one's seniors. One should watch his behavior scrupulously and push himself to seize upon opportunities whenever they present themselves. Provocative behavior toward others should be curbed by the diligent application of willpower. These efforts will lead to opportunities for broader and deeper involvement with the environment (the work situation), and increased anxiety and/or other signs of psychic distress will almost surely appear in persons whose unconscious conflicts have been standing in the way. It is now crucial that one not retreat but instead hold his newly won ground and master the new work involvements. After having mastered the new situation, anxiety will generally subside and further forward steps can be taken. One's worst enemy is self-doubt and fear. One should ask himself, "Do I have the ability and knowledge to do better or undertake a particular task?" If the answer is affirmative, one should *do it*. Not only will there be the immediate reward of the successful act, but this process will further stimulate maturation.

The situation can be considerably more complicated than that which has just been described. Sometimes unconscious conflicts have such a profound impact on the individual's choice of life work that a vocation or profession has been picked which does not permit a living out of the most predominant skills, talents, interests, etc. To follow one's truest inclinations was so forbidden and would evoke such intense anxiety and other symptoms that a choice is made which is the complete opposite of what the person would really like to do or be. These alternative choices are frequently characterized by a lower degree of demand on the person in terms of precision, level of responsibility, commitment, involvement; there is often a lower social value placed on the occupation or field.

What I describe next may be somewhat difficult to follow. Success at a life's work of one's primary choice can represent the *winning* of the forbidden mother (in the case of the boy), or of the father (in the case of a girl). In women, the most common life work to which this formulation applies is making a family. A solution (not resolution) for such burdened people is never to succeed fully or completely in that particular work. In this way they escape guilt and anxiety or worse. Some people who are severely burdened by unconscious conflicts never even get this far. They relinquish their true objectives at the outset; they never choose the field of work for which they are best suited. Instead, they pick a life's work which will be less satisfying and which may at the same time reflect the interests of the parent of the opposite sex. Their choice symbolizes an *identification* with the parent of the opposite sex. By choosing this field, the person never breaks his tie with this parent. It is as if the person has said, "I will give up what I *really* wanted to do and be like the parent of the opposite sex; I will choose a less exacting field which requires less of me and represents the parent of the opposite sex. Now I am not threatened nor do I have to stand alone; I have my mother (or father in the case of a woman) with me."

A program of self-help as outlined may help persons who are not living out their capabilities fully but who are in the field for which they are best suited and are partially successful. Good results are considerably less certain for persons who are failing at work where the choice reflects a deep tie with the parent of the opposite sex. Their psychopathology is much more extensive and will, in all probability, require professional help.

Choice of a career or life's work should be made only after careful reflection about the basis for the interests and one's abilities for the field. Parents should always be willing to help their children make these choices, just as they should be willing to offer assistance with regard to the choice of a mate. The entire course of life may be affected by initial commitment to a vocation, profession, or field of study. Note should be taken of the father's interests and values, and the mother's. Above all, one should recognize what his own talents and most satisfying interests are and pursue those irrespective of the interests of his parents. Just because a boy's father is a businessman does not mean he must be one too, but it could mean that following father's footsteps will bring him the most rewards from life. Assessing the nature of one's adult and ongoing, as well as earlier, relationship to one's parents will provide important clues. A son who has always been closer to his mother, including during his adulthood, who picks a life's work which reflects an interest of his mother (for instance he elects to teach English because his mother was an English major) should think long and hard about the reasons for his choice before he commits himself. His unconscious attachments may be forcing him into his mother's field of interest when his talents and truer interests would be better fulfilled in a different field.

A career other than marriage and making a family provides a common and rather ideal way for a woman to avoid differentiating her femininity fully. By working she has arranged her life circumstances in such a way that her unconscious conflicts surrounding femininity and motherhood can remain relatively dormant. Under these conditions she may be relatively free from psychic distress. Men who avoid marriage are usually troubled by the same problem.

The woman who has begun her family must hold herself to her responsibilities. Unless circumstances force her to work she should not, and if she finds herself anxious, depressed, or otherwise distressed she should first attempt the self-help approach, using her husband

and an older woman for the helping source and, failing
to overcome her difficulties she should seek (good) professional assistance. It is better for her, her husband,
and especially her children, that she become a competent, masterful, and fulfilled woman and mother than
that she turn the care of the children over to a nursemaid. If she cannot effect these changes within herself
by whatever means she uses, she should admit the mistake of ever having attempted motherhood and relegate
the care of her children to a feminine and maternal
nursemaid. If she does not, and continues to force herself into a role which she cannot fill, she will do more
harm than good to herself, her children, and her husband.

Play

Play is an important part of life. Many people who
cannot play successfully may find joy in their work. Persons who have, for justifiable reasons, had to work hard
all of their lives may never have learned how to play,
how to use leisure time. However, there are many whose
conscience is so powerful that they are not permitted the
simple pleasure of play. Without there being a reason
for a particular activity, such as cultivating a business
deal, these people cannot relax, play, and enjoy themselves just for the fun of it. These remarks apply to
sexual pleasure as well.

The primary basis for a joyless life is unconscious
guilt. A guilty orientation to life may receive powerful
social reinforcement in certain religious sects but for the
most part the inability to enjoy life, including play, is
personal and derives from unconscious roots. To be sure,
a person recently or continuously exposed to suffering
mankind or heavy responsibilities or other stress may
not feel like playing, but for the average person forces in
his unconscious are the bases for his lackluster life.
Unconscious forces may directly bar pleasure or they
may act more indirectly by having caused an inhibited
personality, a chronic depression, a slavelike devotion to
work and duty.

When such a pattern is recognized, a determined effort should be made to play. Time should be set aside for leisure activities, and no matter how strong the inner resistance, anxiety, or other reactions, play should be undertaken. An annual vacation should be a part of every life, an event looked forward to and planned and enjoyed. It is incredible how many people cannot enjoy a vacation, not to mention the daily exposure to the beauty of nature around them. It has been said that the family that plays together stays together. I believe there is truth in this saying.

Some people do nothing but play. In such cases play serves as a means for avoiding the responsibilities of maturity. Close inspection into the lives of those who only "play" will reveal that they do not really play. These are miserable people who remain active, often to the point of near-frenzy, as a means by which to avoid the agony of their existence.

Care of the Body

A sure sign of the presence of illness-producing unconscious forces is failure to care for one's body. While some of the reasons for the misuse of the body may derive from the simple lack of knowledge, many people who know better don't do better. Some of the forms of bodily abuse are: failure to care for the teeth, insufficient rest, failure to relax sufficiently and use leisure time well, insufficient exercise, over-eating and improper diet, obesity, failure to follow a physician's instructions when physically ill (the diabetic who doesn't stay on his diet), smoking, excessive use of alcohol and other drugs, ignoring obvious signs of physical disease, and unnecessary risk taking, and so forth. Persons who have enough self-awareness to recognize these and other forms of self-neglect or self-assault should confront themselves and, either on their own strength or on the strength from others, they should change their behavior.

It is remarkable how much anxiety or depression or other frank psychiatric symptomatology will sometimes appear when persons attempt to take better care of their bodies. It is as if their conscience says they do not deserve to be physically healthy, to minimize risks to their well-being or life. Guilt is a prime source for the preceding and other behaviors. Physical health is a precious gift but thousands of persons abuse their bodies, not because of ignorance or poverty but because of forces within their unconscious minds. Some who cannot commit outright suicide do so piecemeal through neglect of their bodies.

Friendship Between Parents and their Adult Children

A serious form of psychopathology, and one which brings heartache to all parties, is the cruel manner in which some young people relate to their parents, and vice versa. While emancipation from parents is a necessary part of the maturational process, many young people rudely cut their parents out of their lives and often, in the process, discard some fine values which their parents have upheld. These reactions reflect any or all of the following: excessive unconscious dependence, hostility, strong incestuous attraction toward the parent of the opposite sex, and the misbelief that identification with the parent of the same sex constitutes a submission or subjugation. Other reasons may exist, deriving from impressions and misbeliefs formed very early in life.

When such attitudes exist toward the parents, the parents should take the initiative and make a sustained effort to break down the wall and establish a good adult relationship with their children. Since the parents are older, hopefully more mature, and still the parents, it is primarily their responsibility to effect the changes.

Many parents and offspring have found each other by both having recognized the distance between them and finding out the reason. I am, in general, opposed to encounter groups and the like because of poor leadership and the tendency for psychological forces to get out of hand. Considerable good, however, can result if the entire family (excluding the very young children) will meet together and explore the basis for their emotional distance. Tempers should remain cool and irrational attitudes should be rigorously searched for. Children of all ages often change their attitudes dramatically when they better understand their parents and the basis for prior behavior. While these clarifications are occurring at a conscious level, and the focus is upon current or past issues not directly linked to repressed childhood conflicts, more will be going on than any of the participants will realize. Unconscious conflicts will be mobilized through these family interactions and the process of conflict resolution and maturation will proceed. I make no claim that such efforts as these will lead to a complete resolution of the unconscious conflicts in any or all, but much can and often will change, enough so that the younger ones may well live a more successful life, and congenial family relations will be established. Parents and offspring should be able to become good friends; when this does not happen something is wrong.

Unfortunately, emotional distance between parents and minor children is frequently associated with destructive behavior on the child's part, such as drug usage, sexual promiscuity, goallessness; in short, the afflictions which are destroying so many of our young people. When talk sessions, as just described, do not suffice then the parents must apply force in the form of very firm control. Punishment will not bring about the desired changes because the destructive behavior in all probability is motivated by an unconscious need for punishment. Parents may have to place the child on house arrest, deprive him of privileges, and deny him access to friends who are sick and destructive. Periodic search of the child's quarters in order to find drugs may be necessary. A careful accounting of the child's financial expenditures should be implemented. If the child reacts violently or threatens to run away, call the police. A show of force has a very sobering effect on the young. Above all, parents, the father in particular, should never fear having a showdown with their offspring and calling a complete halt to the objectionable behavior. Once the tide has turned, the follow-through is an absolute must. After the showdown children will usually be willing to talk. Great effort must then be expended to hold them to a constructive way of life. The show of force is an act of love; children realize that and want it to happen. Turning around a bad situation may take a few weeks or may take months. Persist and never give up. The child is yours to save. Never excuse your child's delinquent or antisocial behavior. Doing so is a way of getting yourself off the hook.

The key is to draw upon the good will of all; let the children emancipate but at the same time all should ferret out and discard irrational attitudes and thus lay the groundwork for an adult relationship for the children. The bonds within the family are priceless; they should extend into adulthood and never weaken.

Homosexuality and Marriage

At this point I wish to state categorically that I do not think homosexuals should ever attempt marriage as a self-help method in hope that doing so will make them heterosexual. Homosexuals are very sick people; they should attempt marriage only after successful psychiatric treatment, and then they should have children only after having given marriage an adequate test of several years. Homosexuals sometimes marry and have children as a cover for their illness.

Homosexuality is as much a public health problem as any of the major diseases which have concerned public officials and the medical profession. It is contrary to nature and represents displacement behavior; the individual displaces onto the same sex what his unconscious conflicts prevent him from expressing with a person of the opposite sex.

I believe it would be better if homosexuals would simply accept the fact that life dealt cruel blows during childhood and that whatever parental urges may exist within them should be sublimated; that is, they should fulfill these urges in other ways and not have children. Little good can come to children from exposure to adults who are so disturbed as to have become overtly homosexual. There are ample means for society to absorb homosexuals without children being involved. For society to permit homosexuals to "marry" homosexuals and adopt children is utter madness.

What I have said about homosexuals applies equally to many others who marry; I refer to persons with psychiatric disturbances of considerable severity. The maladies of many badly disturbed people are not always as easily identified, nor is their natural history or solution as certain. With homosexuals the picture is clear. Find good psychiatric help. Unfortunately, good help is difficult to find. Therefore, the best advice I can give homosexuals who cannot find good treatment or whose efforts to be treated have failed is to accept and learn to live with their illness. Hard facts are hard to face; the fact is that homosexuals can never be good parents. Society owes the confirmed homosexual a place so he can live as full a life as possible, but society must not uphold this way of life to the young as a variant of normality.

Lost Youth

Every generation has had its nonconformists among young people. The ones I have known were very sick people; they were lost and were groping for a way of life which would give them at least a modicum of security. Parents who see their children identifying themselves with any movement which is characterized by extreme non-conformity and non-commitment to a productive way of life should take immediate and decisive steps to prevent further deterioration in the life of their child.

At the first sign of the interest of their child (usually the adolescent) in any aspect of these sick ways of life the parents should confront the child with what they see happening. Nipping the process in the bud is the key. Parents should absolutely prohibit their offspring from associating with persons in these movements. They should not allow their children to don the symbols of these movements. Throw out the posters, search for drugs, and be relentless. I am well aware of how difficult this can or will be, but do it you must. But more than that must be done.

Parents must face themselves squarely and ask how they failed their child in the past so that the child now is inclined to identify himself with a way of life which is nonproductive and/or destructive. They must then more actively involve themselves in the life of their child. Fathers especially must take time to supply the fathering that it is almost certain was lacking during the child's formative years. When this effort is made parents will be appalled by the discovery of how little time they have devoted to their child (or children). The years of neglect or uninvolvement in their child's life will become painfully apparent. It will take great effort on the part of the parents to change their pattern of living with their children. A nondefeatist attitude is absolutely vital. Changing the trend in the young person's life will not happen overnight.

In addition to changing daily living patterns, the entire family should periodically have "family therapy" sessions. Father, mother, and child (or children) should openly discuss what it was in their past history of their lives together that caused the young person to adopt an uncommitted, nonproductive, and usually a destructive way of life. Parents must not be timid about their intrusion into their offspring's way of life.

Parents who do not intervene must question the depth of their love for their child. Unconscious hate in parents toward children can be expressed in a variety of ways. One of the most common is for parents to stand idly by while their child destroys himself. The stance of noninvolvement on the parents' part is explained by them to be a reflection of their respect for the child's individuality, the right to free choice, and other such absurdities. If you really love someone, you don't stand idly by and watch him destroy himself.

It is a mistake to believe parents can improve their relationship with their children by joining their ("cop-out") way of life—by dressing somewhat like they do, trying to become interested in their music, their language—in short, their values. This is the quickest way possible to lose what little may be left of the child's respect for his parent. Remember, the parent, like the doctor, must be committed to the healthy part of the other person, offspring or patient, but must ultimately reject the sick part. It is necessary to try to understand why the sick part developed—in this instance the "cop-out" way of life—but to understand does not mean to accept or endorse what is understood. Understanding sickness is the first step toward removing the condition.

Where decisive intervention and a program of self-help—sessions of "family therapy" and new ways of relating to the child—do not work, then psychiatric treatment must be obtained. Do not hesitate to hospitalize your child if necessary. Arrange for psychotherapy. If you do, look very closely at the personality of the prospective therapist. First have an interview with him to find out what he thinks about the way of life your child has adopted. I know of several professionals who believe present day youth are merely experimenting with new life-styles. Experimenting they are—with ways for destroying themselves outright or with ways to limit their chances for living a full and constructive life.

PART TWO

The Family:
The Source of Social Vitality

Chapter Seven

Careers and the Family

It is in the nature of things for males and females to mate—nothing could be more obvious—but as civilization has evolved, the challenges and opportunities facing men and women have created conditions which seriously undermine family life.

Given the existing economic setup a young man must work to provide for the care of his family. His continuous presence is not as necessary for the proper rearing of *infants and very young children* as is the mother's. A man must be all the more committed to his work after he is married and has a family in order to support them, but he must *not* neglect his family as far too many men do, as they become overly drawn into their jobs or careers, or avoid their family responsibilities for personal reasons.

The future life course of a young woman who does not marry soon after graduating from high school or college is not as simple as it is for the man. The high value placed on an education, and the growing trend for women to work, causes many young women to prepare for a vocation or profession and to embark on a career other than that of making a family. Some expend an enormous amount of time, energy, and money preparing for a career. Sooner or later their urge to mate wins the upper hand, and many working women marry. Marriage

alone does not complicate the life of a young career or
working woman unless her career separates her from
her husband. The problem with so many men and career
women is that when they attempt to make a family,
forces within themselves and the careers to which they
have committed themselves prevent them from doing
this well.

In the past a woman's primary career was marriage
and a family. Now women constitute nearly half of the
work force of the United States. Many of these are young
women who have not married but eventually will; others
are women whose families are grown; some are women
who have not and never will marry; others are widows;
others divorced as a consequence of their own choice,
and all too often because they were abandoned by their
husbands. Unfortunately, tens of thousands of women
who have families and who would prefer to make their
family their career are forced by economic need to go to
work. For an increasing number of women the idea that
having a family is a career of the highest value has
slipped from its former high position, and these women
go to work or develop a career, rather than tend to their
young family. Their children are suffering serious consequences.

With the coming of a child or children, women who
have worked or have had a career in a profession or
vocation are faced with a difficult decision. The decision
to stay at home and care for their child or return to
work soon after the birth of their child confronts all of
them. It is not easy for anyone, man or woman, to stop
working at something he or she has done for many years
and has enjoyed. Much satisfaction comes from the exercise of skills and abilities and the earning of money. To
set aside an entire way of life is not easy. Furthermore,
for men, and women, money may have a special meaning aside from its necessity for daily living.

I have no doubt whatsoever that if the new mother
who has been working is mature and ready for motherhood she will want to, and should, stay home and take
care of her baby. She should remain there at least until

her child goes to school full time. When the child is at school all day it does not matter so much where the mother is, although she should be at home when her child comes home from school. In other words, it is of vital importance for a woman who has a baby to take care of it. Not to do so denies the child the most vital of all human experiences. So-called object constancy (the parent) for infants and young children is extremely important for their personality development. Babies and young children develop best when their mother is present all of the time. (Of course, this statement does not apply to severely disturbed mothers; they should not have had babies in the first place.)

It is equally important for fathers to be constant figures in the young child's life. However, since fathers must be away part of every day, it is imperative that the mother not be away too, during the early years of life. Care in day-care centers can never equal what a mature mother can provide her child. Furthermore, day care centers are often staffed by transient and indifferent personnel. Some baby-sitters are quite good, but even they are no substitute for the continuous presence of a mature mother. I have no wish to make mothers feel guilty for not taking care of their children, but facts are facts, and they should be faced.

Many women who have worked find staying home and caring for their children somewhat difficult in the beginning; they miss the intellectual stimulation and human contact their work provided. They should persevere, because if they are mature enough they will discover that the joys of being a mother and making a home exceed those provided by their job or career. Mature women soon will no longer miss the satisfactions of work, for they are fulfilling their deepest natural instinct, their highest responsibility to nature and to society. I honestly believe that if all mothers ceased caring for their babies civilization would collapse.

Some women who have worked and then begun a family are unable to discover the joys of making a home; in fact, they may suffer great personal strain. Many soon return to work; others stay at home, are miserable, and do a poor job at homemaking and motherhood. Some become so disturbed they eventually require psychiatric treatment.

My strong impression is that a feminine young woman who has matured is unlikely to place a vocation or profession higher in her scale of values than her family. Many women do go to college or work for a few years after graduating from high school. It is not long, however, before they marry and soon abandon aspirations to work. Some very fine and mature young women do have difficulty finding a mate because of personal, physical characteristics or the short supply of men in the area where they live; or they may have taken on responsibilities which force them to continue working. The simple truth is, however, that a mature and feminine woman will usually be married by her mid-twenties, barring unusual circumstances. One cannot categorically say that all unmarried women are not mature. That all women who do marry early or by their mid-twenties are feminine and mature is not true either, of course. Young women may marry for neurotic reasons, that is, for reasons other than a genuine readiness to mate. The reasons include the wish to get away from a miserable home life, a means for finding security, undue concern about the social norm that everybody should marry, a means by which to vicariously live out the role of a male through a husband, the wish to win a "forbidden" man, the urge for a baby, and so on.

Unfortunately, many of the career women who do marry are just feminine and mature enough to be able to marry but not mature enough or feminine enough to make their marriage a complete success, and of course, they tend to choose men who are also short on maturity. This fact accounts in part for the high divorce rate and the fact that many of these women work rather than care for their babies and young children. Some of these women remain at home and live miserable lives and rear their children poorly, thereby contributing to another generation of disturbed individuals. They, and everyone else, would be better off if they did go to work and turn over the care of their children to a more mature woman. Some mothers who continue working would become overtly psychiatrically ill if they gave up working and stayed at home to care for their children. However, everyone would be even better off if these women could receive good psychiatric treatment so they could make a success of their family life.

The woman who embarks on a vocational career must be aware that a significant aspect of her basic nature will go unsatisfied if she never has a family. She should be aware of what she is getting into as she sets her life course. This is no small consideration. Heterosexual commitments and maternalism are powerful needs; to find substitute satisfactions for these biological imperatives can be very difficult and, even if found, a deep sense of bitterness and futility often appears in career women when the opportunity for a family has passed them by.

While I have no proof or evidence based on a large-scale and exhaustive in-depth study of career women, I have treated a sizable number of them, and I have supervised the treatment of many others which was being done by other doctors. These women all share certain obvious characteristics which any observant person can detect. All were dominated by unconscious conflicts which were remarkably similar and which the treatment process exposed.

No one knows what motivates all career and working women, nor have I observed career women in sufficient numbers to claim absolute validity for what I believe about them; however, it is striking how many of them share certain visible characteristics. I am referring to career women with whom I have been acquainted and others of whose treatment I have had knowledge. Their personalities are very similar to those I have known in depth as a result of having treated them. Having made these observations over many years, I believe my inferences about career women are valid. Women who go to work or make a career after their children are in school or their family is grown, and those who are forced to work because of economic need, are strikingly different from many women who have pursued a career without interruption during their adult life.

The one single fact that stands out among all others with regard to the early life of these women and, therefore, with regard to the unconscious conflicts in them, is that some degree of breakdown existed in their relationship with their mothers when they were infants and young girls. During their very early life their mothers either rejected them to some degree or they were excessively anxious with their new responsibilities as a mother. These mothers were themselves not ready to be mothers. Some turned much of the care of their infants over to others; some seemed devoted to their girl babies, but were crippled either by inhibition and other personality difficulties, or followed guidelines which they were taught so as to make it hard for them to fully respond to the needs of their infants.

Furthermore, the mothers of these little girls who never marry and who follow a career instead usually have bad marriages because of their own partial rejection of femininity, and their inability to form a deep and meaningful relationship with a man. Their husbands are frequently not strong men within the family; they may be passive or remote; they may be powerful men in their work but remote or passive in their family. Some were too close to their daughters and may even have been seductive, at times overtly so.

When the mother is not close to her husband, the little daughter gets too close to her father and has difficulty breaking her tie to him, or the opposite occurs. The father is distant and the little girl continually needs warmth from father figures. This unresolved romantic attachment to her father is inevitably associated with envy of the male's way of life. The little girl eventually identifies with her father to one degree or another. The more she identifies with her father, the more she ultimately rejects her mother as a model. Furthermore, her mother never provided a picture of satisfied femininity to her, a fact which caused the little girl to reject a feminine identification all the more.

When young girls who are destined to choose a career for life reach puberty, a single fact emerges; they cannot establish a meaningful and enduring relationship with a young man. Some avoid boys altogether. Some date for a while but eventually give up. Others become homosexual immediately. Some try heterosexuality for a while but either eventually suppress all interest in sexuality or become homosexual. Some carry on in one affair after another but never marry. Some, unfortunately, eventually do marry and have children but never stay at home and care for their children. It is probably better that these women do not care for their children but relegate the care to others. Were such a woman to make the attempt the children would suffer more and the woman might become ill with some form of psychiatric disturbance. It would be much better if such women had never had children in the first place. They should have settled for working out some kind of compatible relationship with their husband and let it go at that.

Subsequent to this troubled period which begins at puberty these young women begin to form an interest in some field or another. They are aware of their inability to successfully relate to a man, and they realize they must do something with their lives. Some simply go to work. If they are fortunate enough to have been endowed with a special talent, high intelligence, or both, they eventually find their way into higher education and a business or professional career. The more deeply they become involved in their vocations or careers, the more fixed they become in their way of life.

What I have written is not condemnatory of these women; they are unfortunate, denied much that life has to give. But many working or career women make substantial contributions to life, and for this they deserve the respect and the rewards due anyone who contributes to society. This statement applies equally to men who never marry but who contribute to society. Most of these men and women, however, suffer silently—and at times not so silently—from some degree of loneliness and awareness that a part of their nature is not being fulfilled. They are missing out on the joys which can only be found within a family of one's own.

Men and Careers

If men are going to father children, they must make time for the child and participate in family life in such a way as to make it possible for the child to grow up into normal manhood or womanhood. There is a difference between the effects on the child when mothers work, and when fathers do. The man who aspires to achieve great heights in his work faces certain hard decisions if he intends to have a family, too. He must inevitably face the decision of how to allocate his time and energy. If he has a family he must not neglect it in the human sense. Children need fathers. It is pointless for a man to devote himself solely to his work, make a fortune, and leave that fortune to his children who will be failures because of inadequate fathering. Such a man may have done society a great service through his career, but he should not have burdened himself with a family, nor should he have imposed personality weakness on his children by depriving them of fathering. Ultimately such children tend to become somewhat of a liability to society.

These remarks should not be understood to mean that a man who is highly successful in his work cannot be a good father also. He must, however, take time to be with his children and his family. Children simply will not develop their full potential if their father rarely involves himself in their lives or fails to organize his family along healthy lines.

The observation has been made that the sons of great men tend not to achieve greatness themselves; in fact, many become total failures. While this pattern does not apply to all sons of great men, the tendency is clearly there. This fact can be used as support for the growing body of evidence that fathers are extremely important for family life and for the best personality development of children. Fathers are just as important as mothers.

I have discussed the incompatibility of the career of motherhood and homemaking and a vocational career. A similar incompatibility exists between fatherhood and a career but in a different way and to a different degree.

It should be obvious that a woman can neglect her children by devoting all of her energies to her house. Some women do just that; they avoid their children just as surely as do career women by attending excessively to physical aspects of the home and neglecting the human beings who live in it. Some men do the same thing by expending all of their energy on their work. The personalities of vast numbers of men have become so emasculated that about all they can do is impregnate their wives and then all but disappear from the scene. They are so weak and ineffectual, so filled with unconscious conflicts, that being a husband, father, and head of the home is way beyond them. Other men are worked nearly to death out of economic necessity and have little energy left over for their family. The jobs of some men take them away from the home for too many hours each day, or for too many days at a time. Men in executive positions or those who own and operate small businesses often become drawn more and more deeply into their work and cannot extricate themselves. Their families rarely see them. Fathers cannot just spend a few minutes a day with their children and expect them to grow into healthy men and women.

I have written very pointedly about women who work. The same advice applies to men. If you are going to invest all of yourself in your work then I think you should not have children. This may be a hard issue for you to face, but face it you must because if you do not, and if you neglect your children and your family life, you will have a heavy millstone around your neck for all of your life. This millstone will be the burden of personal guilt engendered by your perception of having failed your children and family; it will be the enormous drain upon you which will come from attempting to straighten out your poorly adjusted children; it will be financial, for the chances are good that you will have to pay psychiatric bills incurred by the treatment of your children necessitated by any of a great variety of psychiatric disturbances (homosexuality, drug abuse, delinquency, neurosis, psychosis, personality disturbance, and on and on). You will cringe when your children make bad marriages and fail; when they attempt to be successful at their life's work and fail. The chickens always come home to roost, and if you are not a good father the chickens will roost on you.

Think long and hard on the question of whether or not you have what it takes to be a good father and whether you are prepared to order your life in such a way as to make it possible to be one. I said there is no higher calling for a man than to be a good father and head of his family.

I have written at some length about why women avoid the full-time career of motherhood. It is just as distressing, and the consequences are just as serious, when fathers fail as when mothers fail. The reasons for this failing are to be found in the unconscious mind. Men who have had poor fathers usually had poor mothers, too. As a consequence they could not successfully pass through the developmental phases of childhood. Many men can be successful at work but cannot succeed as fathers. Rarely are men successful as fathers but not at work. To step into the role of father and do well usually awakens unconscious conflicts of competition with their father. Furthermore, these men frequently have strong dependency needs which are destined to be frustrated were they to assume the responsibilities of fatherhood. In addition to having to overcome these internal barriers to being a good father at the head of the family, such men are often opposed by their domineering wives who, on the one hand, want their husbands to fill their rightful place but who, on the other hand, oppose them when they attempt to do so.

These unconscious conflicts in men force them to avoid their family responsibilities in several ways. Some men simply refuse to have anything to do with their children when they are at home, spending all of their time at hobbies, in front of the T.V. set, etc. Such a man frequently turns away from his wife as well and often exhibits jealousy toward her because of the time and energy she devotes to her family.

Other men pour all of their energy into their work when they need not do so. They think their long hours at work are necessary, but in reality they are not. Work provides the means for escaping from involvement with their family.

Some men seek the type of work which takes them away from the home most of the week or for longer periods of time. These men become restless and irritable when they are with their families on weekends. In fact, one of the surest signs that a man is troubled by unconscious conflicts is the irritability and moodiness which appears when he is with his family.

Men avoid their families by "going out with the boys," spending time at bars and at other activities which provide the means for escaping from the family. Frequently a mistress occupies much of a man's time which might otherwise be spent much more constructively with his wife and children.

To summarize, men or women who want to have a child but plan to devote most of their time and energy to their career or job (in the absence of economic necessity) have, I think, revealed their unreadiness for parenthood. Such parents should, in my opinion, abandon the idea of having a child rather than abandon the child after having it.

You may continue to mature in the years to come and be ready for parenthood later. If not, you will undoubtedly feel a certain emptiness in your life if you do not have children, but as a consequence of your decision mankind will have fewer psychiatrically disturbed persons—possibly yourself, and almost surely your child sometime in his life. "If you cannot do something well, don't do it," is a good principle to live by; none is more applicable to the rearing of children. They are mankind's most valuable natural resource.

Society must think long and hard about the present trend which places more importance on work and careers than on a high-quality family. Just as serious are those economic conditions which force men to work excessively long work days and force women out of the home and into work. Much attention, support, and prestige is given by society to men and women for their career and work achievement, while practically none is given to those who pursue the most important career of all—the making of a home and a family. *Society had better wake up and provide a great deal more support for those couples who will insure its survival!*

Some Effects of Career Men and Women on Children

Unfortunately, far too many children are exposed to certain kinds of career men and women outside the context of the family. Elementary school teachers are a case in point. Some men and women who have not had children of their own do make excellent teachers and have a good effect on children. This is because there is enough masculinity or femininity and uninhibited paternalism or maternalism in them to be able to live up to the human as well as intellectual demands placed upon them in the classroom. Being a teacher provides an outlet for their parental desires. This situation does not place the kinds of demands upon them that family life does. However, many of the teachers of young children are not masculine or feminine or, if they are, they are not fully comfortable with their gender. Some of these teachers are very hostile toward children. Children who come from healthy families can withstand the effects of such teachers, but little boys and girls who are not so fortunate are having their little personalities polluted even further by such teachers.

Women teachers who have personality disturbances which affect their attitude toward their own gender and toward sexuality frequently try to make sissies out of little boys; they stifle their maleness. Even some women who have had families of their own but who teach while their own children are young, out of choice and not economic necessity, impart unhealthy influences on their pupils as well as their own children. Educators would do society a great service if they would hire only men and women who are good teachers *and* who also have masculine or feminine personalities. Teachers are extremely important, not only as transmitters of knowledge but as stimulants for the development of the personalities of the young. Without realizing it, many serve as substitute parents for small children. Homosexual men and women should never be allowed to teach at the elementary, junior high, and high school levels.

I am appalled by the trend of some teachers to adopt teaching styles and classroom attitudes that minimize the differences between the sexes. This is *wrong*. Children should leave school as educated *boys* and *girls*, not as educated sexless beings or confused about sex-role differences. Take a close look at educators who advocate these new trends in blurring sex role differences between boys and girls in the nursery and classroom, and you will see women who are not fully feminine and men who are not fully masculine. Their personalities and values influence the young in school, just as the personalities and values of parents influence children in the family. Sex-role differences should be enhanced, not blurred, in all settings. Ideally, those who influence the young, be they parents, doctors, or other career persons, should be as mature as possible. Unfortunately, many are not.

Professional people have marked impact on society and while a single psychiatrist cannot do much about this I hope you will, after reading this book, keep a close watch on the effects society (and this frequently refers to career women and men) has on you, and especially on your children. Parents can and should influence their school boards to select teachers who will bring out the best in children. Parents should refuse to let their children wear unisex clothing or clothing which reverses the appearance of the sexes. Parents can bring pressure to bear on university teachers who uphold certain values as the new "norm" for society. There are professors in the humanities and other career persons who endorse new life-styles (sex blurring, open marriage, role reversal in the family, etc.) without any factual basis for doing so. One woman psychologist I know is teaching her class that it is perfectly normal for the father to stay at home and care for the children while the mother works and makes the living. Such a claim is irresponsible and destructive. Teachers who make such claims have overstepped their perogatives. Their responsibility is to inform their students, not to openly advocate changes in life-styles in the absence of substantial evidence for the validity of their point of view.

I cannot make a general statement about the personalities of all teachers, university professors, and authors who advocate the new life-styles—unisex, homosexuality, swinging, open marriage, mate swapping, communal living, etc.—but I invite you to look closely at their personalities. I predict you will find the women to be aggressive, domineering, and somewhat masculinized (or at least unfeminine); and the men somewhat short on masculinity. I know this for certain: these self-proclaimed authorities who often say the traditional family is obsolete and that traditional male and female differences are spurious have no scientific basis for their claims and are expressing nothing more than personal opinions. Unfortunately, their academic rank or notoriety as authors places a certain stamp of authority on their pronouncements. Look into their parental history, look into their own family patterns (if they are married), look at their children, and I think you will have little trouble deciding that these individuals have disturbed personalities. I believe these individuals are recommending for mankind ways of life which they have found to take the strain off their own disturbed personalities.

It could be argued that I have no right to endorse certain human values and not others. But if mature psychiatrists do not have some knowledge of what is good for people, I don't know who does. It is our business to know; that is what psychiatry is all about. The evidence is overwhelming that certain kinds of parents and family patterns produce children who become strong men and women, and that other parents and family patterns produce sick children, or children who will become sick or ineffectual when they reach adulthood. These sick patterns in the family produce certain kinds of people who endorse some of the values of which I am so critical. These values become transmitted to the young and to society in a variety of ways—through music, clothing styles, schools and universities, movies, literature and television, and more directly through interpersonal contact.

I urge you not to accept everything that is being promoted these days by professionals and self-proclaimed authorities whose values reflect their disturbed personalities. Fathers and mothers must stand shoulder to shoulder against many of the current influences on their children. It is your obligation as a parent to protect your offspring from harmful, polluting influences. The human spirit can be polluted just as the environment can. Keep an eye on society and on the professionals and oppose them if you see their influence making your children less responsible, competent and masterful masculine boys and feminine girls. Far too many parents have thrown up their hands in despair and have let sick forces in society swallow their children.

The efforts of parents to protect their children will not succeed in every instance because many young people are beyond being influenced constructively. However, you should know that all children and adolescents want their parents to be strong and to set reasonable limits and uphold valid values. Young people often react initially with loud protests and tend thereby to frighten and discourage their parents, but parents should stand firm and hold their ground. *You* set the guidelines and uphold the best values; you can no longer fully rely on the institutions of society to do this for you.

It is my hope that this chapter will help you recognize all the more clearly the necessity for making your family (if you have one) your primary career. Not to do so may cost you and society dearly. When your family disintegrates, all else in life tends to slip, too.

Chapter Eight

The Destruction of America

It seems to me increasing numbers of men and women are psychologically castrated and naturally their families, if they attempt family life, are castrated. That is, male and female identities and roles are becoming increasingly blurred, personal effectiveness is thereby diminished, and the products of such castrated families will be crippled in one or more of a variety of ways.

In this part the focus will be on the relationship between the individual and society, its values and institutions. The family is the only intervening link between the individual and society. The events within the family, the personalities of the parents, the way they relate to each other and to their children—all are pivotal points around which civilization turns. The crisis extends to the very roots of our country. Much needs to be done at both the social and individual levels to revitalize America. Profound changes in our social structure, certain laws and in the quality of people we are producing with each successive generation are now in process.

These difficulties began with the coming of the industrial age. Wars and economic pressures have played their part as well. The key element leading to the "castration" of men, women, and families has been the progressive removal of the man from his family. As a consequence, children have been increasingly denied the psy-

chological growth-promoting effect of the presence of an
involved, loving, and masculine father. His absence placed
many additional burdens on the mother which by necessity took her away from her children. Over the years,
wars, economic pressures, the trend toward material-
ism, the lowered quality of family life in large cities, and
long commuting distances for fathers have removed men
from the home and lowered the quality of family life.
The cost has been enormous. Women have had an additional dilemma to deal with. Ways of life other than
homemaking have become steadily more available to
them. With men away, and staggered by the additional
burdens on them, small wonder the grass has tended to
look greener outside the home, especially so when their
own readiness for a heterosexual commitment and homemaking has been progressively diminished. This occurred
as a consequence of absent fathers and overburdened
mothers when they were developing little girls, or as
adults whose husbands tend to be away so much of the
time.

Currently, many men simply abdicate their leadership position in the family, and as consequences women
have been forced to become heads of families, or families
simply fall apart. Because of the impact of these changes
in role function and family stability, characterologic
changes have taken place in children so that with the
coming of each generation men have tended to become
progressively less responsible and more passive, retir-
ing—even effeminate—and women more domineering and
aggressive and masculinized. These are *psychological*
changes which are contrary to Nature—women's lib
movement notwithstanding—and create a contradiction
within the individual which not only leads to personal
suffering and diminished effectiveness, but virtually in-
sures stresses and strains in heterosexual relationships.
Men and women tend to compete with each other rather
than live out the marvelous harmony which Nature provides for.

The inability to cooperate, interpersonal competitiveness, irresponsibility, dependence, and passivity in the

male, and competitive, masculine strivings in the female used to be seen in isolated instances within couples. Now these personal patterns are becoming national patterns. These masses of individuals inevitably and by personal necessity reorder social values. The making of families and the care of children assume a low priority. It is so because people create ways of living which permit them to find a reasonably comfortable fit with the environment. For instance, the more outspoken leaders of the feminist (this term is a misnomer) movement rarely speak of the importance of homemaking, being a mother and wife. Instead, they champion life-styles which, when examined closely, reveal an underlying envy of the male, a desire to do what he does, indeed to be like him, and at times a deep hostility toward him. A glaring example is the pressure being exerted by the gay lib movement to have their way of life accepted as normal.

It should be recalled that in the early days of the Roman Empire the family was a solid unit with the man at its head. He had absolute authority and commanded great respect. The Roman wife was a magnificent, highly spirited woman, not weak, but strong in the best feminine sense of the word. These families produced the great empire. But the men were taken away as Roman legions expanded the boundaries of the empire and slowly but surely the Roman family changed. The women became "emancipated," families disintegrated, homosexuality flourished. Secret cults sprang up of "women-men and men-women" (homosexuals), whose activities centered on the literal ritualistic castration and destruction of young males; decay was everywhere; sexuality was unrestrained and eventually the empire collapsed. A thousand years of dark ages followed. What is happening in America has happened before.

I have been frequently reminded of the fact that those psychiatric truths about which I have written on family life are clearly described in the Bible. That observations from a psychiatric vantage point should so closely parallel scripture is interesting indeed. Theologians will interpret this finding as evidence of God's work. Those working within a purely scientific framework will see an element of cross-validation in the parallel.

I believe it is now absolutely safe to conclude that it is axiomatic that mature men who by definition are masculine, and mature women who by definition are feminine can make families which produce healthy children who become strong men and women. Such individuals made America great. They imposed their strong will on the land and developed the greatest nation of all time.

Now, progressively fewer people can make families and many families that do exist are very sick families or they fall apart. Our land is being flooded by sick people with the coming of each generation. Our values are changing, our laws will change and down we go. Ours is still a great country, but our Constitution, the Bill of Rights, our laws, traditions, and institutions which have made us great and the leading nation in the world will continue to do so only if the individuals within the land are strong and have the opportunity to find personal fulfillment within the framework of our traditions and values. Consider some of the changes which are taking place in America.

Alcoholism and drug use are virtually at an epidemic level. While it is true that drugs and alcohol have direct habituating and addictive effects, the primary reason people ingest chemicals is to calm their anxiety or remove depression. It is no mystery why millions of our youth are using drugs. They are psychologically unready to master the challenges of life. Instead of looking to the future with anticipation and joy, they are fearful of experiencing a sense of defeat. They turn to chemicals to calm or energize themselves. The annual multi-billion-dollar street drug business in our country is a shocking and alarming barometer of the psychological condition of millions of our fellow Americans. Without access to marijuana, cocaine, heroin, and other drugs, millions of Americans, most of whom are youthful, would have to face reality and/or ask for help rather than take the easier, retrogressive, escapist route. Drug pushers are criminals of the worst kind; they profit from human weakness and illness and, along with the sick users, are seriously damaging our society. Study after study reveals serious family disturbances in the drug user—not in all, to be sure, but in most of them.[1] Even healthy people can get hooked on drugs; this fact shows what powerful and destructive substances drugs are. The damage to the individuals who use drugs and the damage they in turn do to society through lowered efficiency is enormous.

When drugs fail, suicide is the final step in the admission of defeat. Suicide is now the second or third most common cause of death of the young. On the threshold of life many of our young people are ending their lives. This phenomenon is not surprising; in fact, it is predictable in view of the disintegration of the family. These desperate young people lack the inner resources to face life, and master it.

Child abuse and spouse abuse have become a national disgrace. The American family has recently been defined as one of the most violent places on earth. Physical and sexual assaults have reached a shocking level. These phenomena are not mysterious. The abuser was abused and neglected as a child. As an adult he lacks the patience required of parents. The sexual molester failed to mature psychosexually. The root causes stand out in sharp relief when a retrospective study is made of these violent and abusive individuals. This trend can be expected to increase.

School violence is so bad, what with rape and assault on teachers, that a new syndrome—combat neurosis for school teachers—has been proposed. Droves of our best teachers are resigning because of the chaos in the classroom. These violent children are enraged, primarily because of the deprivations within the context of their family life, and only secondarily because of the social conditions in which they live. Furthermore, lacking an inner authority, they even murder the most benevolent external authority—the school teacher.

The quest for excellence is no longer the burning desire of many young people (or many older ones for that matter) it once was. Our universities, the storehouses and propagators of the best in man's knowledge and achievement, have become infested by a sickness that is tragic. While there are still pockets of excellence in centers of learning, the overall quality of the university experience has declined as well as the level of intellectual development of those entering universities, as has been shown by recent surveys. Even our service academies are having trouble with the honor systems. Now college campuses are hotbeds of drug usage, free-swinging life-styles; many students have a complete disregard for our best traditions. Students tend to show less regard for personal appearance. Particularly appalling is the appearance of some medical students and young doctors, especially those who enter psychiatry. Now many of these young professionals are shabby and in no way reflect those qualities of self-respect, reliability, responsibility, and competence which provide the very foundation for the field of medicine. This is an especially ominous sign, for physicians have traditionally reflected the highest values of society. Some of the professors at both undergraduate and graduate level, especially in personal appearance, are not limited to the universities. Look on the streets.

Huge members of youth are absolutely lost. They literally do not know who they are; they lack goals; they find oblivion in drugs and other forms of escapism; they don't know where to go and, if they knew, they lack the personal resources of self-confidence and masterfulness which would make it possible for them to get there. Pot smoking, by twenty million Americans, is part of this decline. Make no mistake—marijuana contains a very toxic substance. Its regular usage favors retrogression, flight, apathy, the very last kind of human qualities people need in these uncertain times. Many young people have no respect for authority and little regard for the effects of their behavior on others. Their aim appears to be to eliminate what was established by past generations. They seem not to comprehend the great effort it has taken to build this country and how necessary are the values and institutions which give it support and strength and stability. They no longer accept the values that have made this a strong and stable society. The effects on our society of these hundreds of thousands of young people defies estimation. Moral decay is like an abscess in the vital organs of a man.

The flourishing pornography business provides one of the most ominous barometers of the state of emotional health of millions of Americans. Emotional health is achieved through proper childhood development in a healthy family. Conversely, emotional disturbances of which psychosexual disorders are a major component, are a product of disturbed home life. X-rated movies and pornography rarely depict mature sexuality. Pornography depicts the perversions and the debasement of women, and this business flourishes simply because of its wide and increasing appeal to millions of Americans.

A particularly ominous sign of our times is the blurring of the differences between male and female, the psychological "castration" to which I have referred. Even Doctor Spock has deleted references to boys and girls in his new book! Anyone who will take the time to observe will immediately recognize this blurring. Charles Winick provides a shocking description of how extensive these changes are in his book, *The New People: Desexualization in American Life*.[2] These changes have also been demonstrated by means of in-depth psychological testing. Winick has pointed out that, in most of those societies which eventually died out and about which knowledge exists regarding the reasons for their decline, sex-role blurring existed.

It is important to recall that Cicero scathingly attacked the pronounced effeminacy of young Roman male aristocrats; no doubt he realized the Roman empire was doomed with such males inheriting positions of leadership. The painful truth is that sex role definition in our young people is less defined now than thirty years ago. The changes are like a plague sweeping the country.

While the individuals themselves are not perishing, their spirits are. These weak people along with others who are weakened in other ways will inherit our land.

Add up all of these changes: increase in crime; mental illnesses, in both adults and children; suicide, the second largest cause of death in young people; alcoholism; drug usage (of epidemic proportion); child abuse (one million instances annually)! In fact, the family is described in a recent study as the most violent place in America; high divorce rate with eight and one-half million children being reared in a single-parent home; juvenile crime; increase in crime among women; minimal restraint on sexuality; decrease in educational achievement in young people; severe sex-role blurring; increase in homosexuality and acceptance of this condition as normal; decrease in parental authority; lowered influence of the church; disregard for all authority by many young people; corruption at all social levels, including an erosion of integrity in high office; the return of scabies and lice (diseases of the dark ages); uncontrollable increase in venereal disease, including AIDS, a large portion of which is transmitted by homosexual acts and by youth as young as twelve-years-old; a general decline in the quest for excellence especially among the young; disregard for personal appearance including those in positions of responsibility; the absence of national heroes for the young to emulate; the confusion about equal opportunity and equal ability with the associated diminution of quality—and look at the total. All of this spells a serious deterioration in this wonderful nation.

However, the problem does not end there; individual decline does not exist in a vacuum. Society reinforces what is happening to individuals and groups of individuals. Social reinforcement occurs in several ways: (1) individuals of like kind band together and form social movements; (2) leaders of these movements appear from within these groups; (3) society eventually endorses some of these movements by writing new laws. The unsuspecting, uninformed, and the weak give their approval to that which is proposed by the leaders of these movements and we must abide by new laws whether we like it or not.

For instance, the militant feminists are, in my opinion, driven to a large extent by motivations from within their own personalities more than by rational considerations. People usually try to alter the environment to suit their personalities rather than change (mature) in order to be able to meet the challenges and expectations of a mature adjustment. Many of these militant leaders have not been successful in their marriages or as mothers—if they ever married—and some are admittedly homosexual. Furthermore, they enlist the "authority" of renowned professionals to endorse their movements. Margaret Mead, for instance, not only was in the forefront of the women's liberation movement, but she also said that bisexuality should be considered normal. She endorsed a "marriage" by two homosexual women, and their claim that they can be adequate parents to five children.

There are many inequities in our society; however, it remains to be seen whether the women's liberation movement and equal rights legislative efforts do more harm than good overall.

Another example of social reinforcement of personal psychopathology can be found in the formal position taken by the American Psychiatric Association and the American Psychological Association; that homosexuality is merely a variant of sexuality, rather than a form of psychopathology. Bear in mind, however, that many psychiatrists and psychologists clearly understand the true nature of homosexuality and opposed the formal position which was taken by these two associations.

How could this incredible declaration by the two major mental health professions have come about? The answer is not difficult to find. Men and women who enter the mental health professions are very commonly troubled within themselves. This fact is well known. As a result, they tend to be sympathetic toward the social aspirations of disturbed persons. Furthermore, mental health personnel tend to consider the individual before society.

As a consequence, when faced by strong lobbying pressures they are more likely to back down rather than stand firm. Our Congress and certain national leaders have demonstrated a similar weakness and as a consequence women are filling positions that only men should fill. There is a certain "sympathy" in the more disturbed mental health professionals for homosexuals and from this sympathy comes the mistaken belief that a kindness is being done when they ask society to accept these persons as "normal."

Homosexuality is not biologically caused. The causes are to be found in childhood development within the context of disturbed family life. Typically the father is weak or absent and the mother is overly possessive, domineering, or insecure. Wars always cause a crop of homosexuals because fathers are away. The condition is increasing in prevalence and will continue to do so. Rampant homosexuality is one of the signs of societies in crisis or in a state of collapse. The gay movement is an extremely ominous sign because of the significance of the phenomenon. Equally ominous is the remarkable success the gays are having in convincing segments of our society that theirs is a normal condition. Fortunately, clear-thinking and healthy people have not yielded to this propaganda. Even so, homosexual values are finding their way into schools, including medical schools, books, even into the courts (as when a homosexual was appointed a Superior Court Judge), and into the very fabric of our culture, alongside the unisex propaganda that boys and girls are essentially the same.

There exists no clearer example of how individual psychopathology leads to social pathology. A key element in the gay banner is the view that bisexuality is the norm, not heterosexuality. While you and I are immune to this poisonous propaganda, the vulnerable young are not. It is appalling to see so many school teachers subscribe to these views. The laws of Nature are strong, but man has the capacity to override them, and when he does he destroys himself. The so-called "normalization" of homosexuality, and the obliteration of the differences between the sexes are the major elements in the destructive processes now underway.

The most alarming sign of social decay is the reappraisal of the meaning of incest and what society's response should be to it. In Sweden an attempt was made to decriminalize incest. In the United States a certain social worker is leading a "movement" to re-examine the phenomenon. He claims that all incest may not be bad, and that the child is not necessarily harmed by parent-child sexual relations.[3]

The two most fundamental taboos of civilization are cannibalism and incest. The reasons should be obvious to every thinking person. The prohibition of sexual relations within families is a key element in personality development and the civilizing process. The very fact that serious consideration is being given to adopting a permissive attitude toward incest is unquestionably the most serious sign of all with regard to the decay of our society.

The abolition of the incest taboo would be the endpoint of the current trend in society toward ever greater direct gratification of the instinctual side of life. Some gratification is, of course, necessary, but much of our instinct and energy forms the basis for the creative process and cultural development. Cultural growth is lagging, the quest for excellence is disappearing—predictably—as the instincts and the senses are ever more directly gratified through drugs, freewheeling sexual styles, pornography and near-pornographic movies, plays and publications, homosexuality, child prostitution, an overall decline in morality, and now, possibly, God forbid, incest itself.

The laws of the land *are* changing as a consequence of these various social movements and the overall quality of life will suffer as a consequence. The fine concept of equal opportunity for everyone is being mistreated as meaning that everyone is equal. They are not. Men and women are not equal in ability. They are equal in worth but their worth will only be fully realized by *enhancing*, not *blurring*, their differences. Among men inequality exists; the same holds for women. Greatness for a society can only come when individual differences are recognized, outlets for expression provided, and high performance rewarded.

Viewing any of these developments in isolation fails to reveal the big picture. The tendency is to brush off swinging sexual styles as a passing fad, or the "normalization" of homosexuality as a transient event which will in time pass away, or pornography as harmless if you do not let your children get hooked, or the re-evaluation of incest as the workings of the misguided mind of a kook, etc. By lumping all these moral developments together, by backing off and viewing them from a distance, *and* by looking into the psychopathology in the personalities of those who embrace the developments (in particular their champions), *then* you begin to really see and understand the extent of our disintegration. Some brush all this aside and claim that the next generation will clear all this up, assuming, with this claim, that wisdom and emotional health automatically appear with every new generation. They do not.

The picture is clear. Personal psychopathology has led to social pathology and laws are being passed which reinforce personal and social pathology. Remove legal restraints against possession of marijuana, tie the hands of the authority, pass laws which reinforce the blurring of the differences between males and females, and turn us into a homogeneous, unisex society. Permit the most depraved behaviors to appear on the screen, TV, and on the street, and encourage the care of children by nonparents rather than reward those who make families and head homes, let women do jobs that men do better, keep pulling the props out from under the family, etc., and the demise of this great country will be assured.

The time has come for individuals to take a strong defensive stand against the trends that are rushing our great country to destruction. Individuals must act first in their own self-interest and make a start somewhere. By so doing, we all collectively may save our way of life.

Chapter Nine

Unisexism and the Women's Movement

Today we are seeing the character of men and women change very drastically from the clearly established male and female identities of times past toward unisexism or downright role reversal. The increase in homosexuality is part of this trend. Fortunately some men and women have escaped it, but many have not, and I believe the trend will worsen before it gets better, *if* it ever does. If the trend continues, our society is doomed; sexual identity blurring always weakens the durability of the male-female bond and the capacity to form a family.

Imposing the unisex values on developing children is harmful to them, yet that is exactly what is happening in America today. This is probably one of the most destructive influences of our times on our children and young adults. In schools at all levels "experts" in sociology, psychology, and even some biologists are taking the position that the differences between the sexes have been overemphasized. The textbooks for small children are being rewritten so as to obscure and even erase references to boy, girl, and role preferences which the sexes have found congenial in times past.

The federal government is eliminating references to male and female in government regulations, directives, and guidelines. Schools that receive federal aid are prohibited from restricting females from certain male activities, mostly sports. The armed forces are being forced to permit women to enter many areas of activity that men have exclusively occupied. The Labor Department has decreed quotas for women in heavy industry. All of these events are happening under the guiding concept of equal rights and equal opportunity acts. This trend all adds up to the point of view that a man and woman are virtually interchangeable in context, that there is no difference between male and female.

The fact of the matter is that there are enormous differences between male and female by all the methods of analysis and measurement, including the most obvious—simple, direct observation.

Differences exist between male and female in their anatomy, in the cells, in the hormones, in their chromosomes, in their tissues, in how they metabolize food, and in their mental makeup. In doing research of *any kind* the most fundamental control that must be introduced in the design of the research is the separation of subjects to be studied on the basis of sex. Psychological tests in particular must control for sex. Men, women, boys, and girls are more susceptible to different diseases. On the average, women are 40 percent less physically strong than men. Women relate to babies and children entirely differently than do men; not to be overlooked is the fact that women have babies, and have breasts with which to nurse them, and the temperament to find these experiences profoundly satisfying. Maternalism and paternalism are different human qualities.

Yet despite these profound and extensive differences between male and female our society has gotten to the point that our young are being taught that they are not different (male vs. female), and that sexual identity and sexual role preference has been forced upon our forebears, and on them through a process of social conditioning designed by men primarily for the exploitation of women.

Not many years ago a Russian scientist imposed the Communist doctrine (which claims we are what we are because of social influences) on his botanical research. Unfortunately for him, but fortunately for the rest of us, the laws of Nature were powerful enough to withstand his tinkering, and he was proven to be a fraud. In time, unisexists, sociologists, psychologists, etc. who peddle the unisex line, which claims women have been conditioned to their position in life by evil male chauvinists, will be just as roundly discredited.

While the human intellect or spirit enjoys great plasticity and is highly adaptive, it is sheer blindness to fail to see the connection between our mind and our body. The quality of a tree and a bush is different because of their structural differences. A rose is a rose and not a daisy because of the wide range of structural differences that appear with every type of measurement and analysis. The overall differences between male and female are best described by poets and artists; the individual differences are as profound as they are necessary and can be demonstrated scientifically.

In addition to the differences between the sexes there are a wide range of differences between individuals within each sex. Every parent, in particular the mother, will tell you each of her children was different at birth. The art of parenting is to detect the differences in babies and foster the unfolding of the great potential that lies dormant in their biology. No potential is of more profound importance then the child's maleness or femaleness. No single environmental influence does more damage to the developing human spirit than[1] to impose the wrong psychological sexual identity on the biological imperative of the child.

It is true, because of man's adaptability, that the individual can force himself to *behave* in ways that are not in harmony with his basic qualities. To do so always produces strain that damages both the psychology and physiology of the individual. A male who is forced by his childhood development to acquire the psychological identity of a female and live out that identity is in a profound state of internal conflict. The same applies to the female. Similarly, men and women whose psychology is in harmony with their biology, but who are forced by necessity or social pressure to live out a social role which is contrary to their basic makeup produces conflict and strain.

There is no more sure way for parents and others to impair the psychological development of children than to effeminize boys and to masculinize girls. Powerful social forces are at work, however, which push parents in that direction.

People who are not in conflict psychologically, and this also means they are not in conflict with what they are biologically, usually manage to find a place for themselves in society if they are given the freedom to do so. Great social pressure exists today which in effect robs young men and women of their freedom of choice. The impact of laws such as Title IX or the Equal Opportunity Act which provide for freedom of choice on the young is vastly different than social movements which use these laws to further their own aims. The effect on young women and on society of the freedom for women to enter heavy industry is very different from social pressure which proclaims that true "personhood" can only be found if women enter these fields of endeavor.

There is no question that women have been discriminated against. They have had no spokesman or organization to look after their interests. In the free market it is inevitable that they would be exploited, that is, the effort would be made to get as much out of them for as little as possible. But this process is not unique to women. Men have exploited other men (and boys) for centuries. Getting as much for as little as possible is the name of the game. Social processes are at work which are correcting these inequities, injustices, and prejudices against women and much progress has been made. To this end the Women's Liberation movement has had a very constructive effect on our way of life. Many inequities remain, however, for *both* men and women; it will be a long time before the best possible reward system is worked out for what the individual contributes to society.

In addition to the time-freeing effect modernization has had for women, the ravages of inflation have forced many women into the work force who otherwise would have preferred to stay at home. Many of these women are untrained, and, therefore, by necessity must accept lower-paying positions, a fact which appears discriminatory when their income and positions are fed into the statistics, but in reality is not. Their finest skills are expressed in the home, but they are forced out into the work force by economic need. *That* is discriminatory.

One of the battle cries of the feminists is this very point—if women did not spend so much time making families, they would not lose out in the work force; they would not be handicapped by having been out of the running.

One solution of the women's liberationists' (at least of some of them) is to divide up child care equally. Soon after the birth of the child, they propose that the woman and man should share equally in the child's care. By each working half-time at their jobs, the infant and child would receive equal amounts of parenting from both mother and father. By this method the woman would not lose out in the work force.

It is quite true that both parents are necessary for the best possible psychological development for the child. However, the importance of mothering and fathering vary at different stages of the child's development (see chapter 2).

Some parents believe the infant or small baby can be turned over to a caretaker or day-care center so they can return to their work. They cite studies which purport to show that children develop just as well in these situations, as those who are reared by full-time parents. Measuring human qualities is very difficult; particularly the capacity to love, to be committed to people and to work, to be masterful and so forth.

These few paragraphs have introduced the destructive aspects of the Women's Liberation movement. In their rush to enter the labor force they are literally throwing the baby out with the bath. They are losing sight of the absolutely essential place the family has for mankind. It appears as if they do not believe the family is important, or if it has some importance, it ranks low in the scale. How can this be? The question to be addressed is why have women turned away from the home in such large numbers. Why are so many women becoming hostile toward men, so competitive with them, and so envious of the social role men have traditionally filled? Why are men so meekly standing aside? Bear in mind that men are turning away from marital and family responsibilities too, but they are less visible because their "Men's Liberation Movement" organization is just beginning.

Extensive research has demonstrated differences between male and female across a wide range of measurements. Obviously the sexual anatomy is different, and so is the reproductive function. There are marked hormonal differences, the chromosomes are different, bone structures, body size and strength differ, and brain differences have been described. Sex can be determined by looking at hair under the microscope, total body fat and distribution is different, and the thickness of skin differs. Psychologically, the clear difference in aggressiveness has been repeatedly observed. Intellectual differences appear at puberty.

Psychological tests reveal some very fundamental differences with regard to how individuals relate to the environment. In fact, any scientific investigator who submitted a research proposal to fellow scientists would be the laughing-stock of the scientific community if he took issue with the absolute necessity to separate his subjects on the basis of sex. Distinction of research subjects on the basis of sex is probably the most fundamental step the scientist must take before proceeding with his work. Male and female simply are profoundly different— and thank Heaven for the differences! The claim that women are the way they are because of age-old discrimination is nonsense.[2]

Societies have evolved in such a way as to permit a comfortable articulation between the psychological qualities of the man and woman and their biological underpinnings. There are, to be sure, areas of overlap between men and women. Both share certain physical and psychological qualities and, indeed, there are tasks in life to which either sex can adapt and which either sex can master, and where they can, they should be rewarded equally. Most people believe the equal pay for equal work concept is proper. I certainly do.

Society recognizes these shared propensities and capabilities and has opened the door wide to both sexes in many areas of life. This is as it should be. There are, however, substantial differences between male and female, and society must provide for these differences, capitalize on them, and reward them wisely. Not only does the individual find peace of mind and fulfillment when he finds his proper fit in the environment, but society gets the most out of the individual. Obviously society must also provide for a continual source of new life which can fully express itself and breathe life into the values, customs, laws, traditions, etc. which define the society and move it forward. This source of new life is, and can only be, the family. Clearly, therefore, a large proportion of individuals of any society must be able to create new life and launch it well, that is to say, we *must see to it* that most of our citizens have the capacity to make families and be good parents. This is a fundamental, inescapable requirement for a society to survive, and especially for it to flourish.

Men who are psychologically troubled have an easy way out from their family responsibilities for society has always expected the male to man the work force. The psychologically troubled male does not need a "liberation" movement; society provides one for him. Married men get away from their family responsibilities by going to work every day, and often the great dedication men show for their work is also a disguised means for escaping from family responsibilities which they cannot master because of psychological disturbances within. These disturbances generally lie relatively dormant as long as they are not triggered by too close a relationship with their wives or children.

Psychologically troubled women similarly have to get away from (be liberated from) homemaking and maternal responsibilities when their psychological conflicts are activated by these responsibilities, or the prospect of marriage. This is what the term "liberation" really refers to. Obviously these women have to do something with their lives and they do. Some never marry, some live with men (or women), some marry and never have children; some marry, become mothers and promptly go to work outside the home; some remain at home and develop some form of manifest psychiatric illness. Some become the militant champions of the women's liberation movement and impose their value system on the banner of that movement.

Emotionally healthy women whose finances are adequate generally remain at home and provide the highest possible gift to the child—mothering, at least until the child starts going to school. She and her husband provide healthy family life which prepares the young for the next cycle. There are, of course, many psychologically healthy men and women who elect, for one reason or another, not to marry and become parents.

While it is true that vast numbers of women with children are forced to go to work out of financial necessity and that many gifted and skilled and trained women quite naturally return to work after their children have started school, I believe a major element of the women's liberation movement originates from another source.

The statement of one of the militant women liberationists—I did not use the term *feminist* because I do not see true femininity within the extreme and militant elements of that movement—captures a major motivation behind the movement. "We are becoming the men we wanted to marry" makes glaringly obvious the so-called "masculinity complex" in the banner of the Women's Liberation movement. This complex and its corollary, the "antifemininity complex," as manifested by those feminine women who are too anxious or timid to fulfill themselves within the context of a family of their own, are the products of developmental disturbances during childhood. These women have little choice but to alter society's values and its fabric so as to find a comfortable niche for themselves in the environment. Do not hear me as being critical of them; they are doing what they have to do.

These women (and their male counterparts who abandon their family responsibilities) are the product of several generations of disturbed family life. They are a reflection of the trend that began about eighty-five years ago. They did not receive the quality (or quantity) of parenting necessary to make it possible for them to live in harmony with a member of the opposite sex and create a family. This fact is *not their fault*, nor is it the fault of their parents, or their grandparents. All were caught in a complex of social and individual interactions which disturbed their psychological development as children. They did the best they could and passed on their qualities to their children, and so on. But here is the grave danger for the future of society: when the number of these individuals is sufficiently large, society will collapse simply because too few real families exist.

The inequities for women will eventually be corrected without this faction within the Women's Liberation movement, just as inequities among men have been eliminated throughout our history and are still being addressed. The feminists' insistence that reference to sexual differences be removed from school books, government regulations, etc., their obvious quest for the man's way of life rather then enhancement of what females do best, their promotion of so-called assertive groups (which in truth teach competition rather than harmony between the sexes), their open acceptance of the lesbian influence, etc., are the unfortunate aspects of the Women's Liberation movement. These elements within the movement are expressions of the psychopathology which I have been describing, the consequences of which are highly destructive. This faction is having its way, and our male lawmakers tremble in their presence like small boys facing a wrathful mother.

All of these alterations in our way of life reinforce the trend toward unisexism and mediocrity, and contribute to the leveling process in our country. Whenever an individual cannot fill the place where his talents and abilities are best expressed, efficiency drops. Mixing the sexes as if they were equals in all respects will lower the efficiency of the particular organization. Society must reappraise the value of what women do best, upgrade the rewards and encourage the woman to develop her femininity and associated skills rather than reward her quest for the male identity and role. Furthermore, the mixing of the sexes in close quarters for prolonged periods of time disrupts male-male bonding and often creates new liaisons between male and female which disrupt the family commitment to which each should remain faithful. Sailors' wives do not like it one bit that women are going to sea with their men. They understand human nature.

Women are being forced out of the home by the ravages of inflation; others are being lured away by the false values of the Women's Liberation movement, which proclaims doing your own thing outside the home is paramount in importance. Like it or not, the movement both implicitly and explicitly espouses competition and rivalry between the sexes.

Lost in this massive reordering of our way of life is the basic truth that children must have parents. Elements within various mental health professional groups and a variety of self-appointed experts are proclaiming that almost any cluster of individuals qualifies as a family, that caretaker arrangements are as good as family life. Fundamental truths about the human condition are being blindly pushed aside.

Current laws provide equal opportunity for women, as well as certain guaranteed rights and protection. These special provisions for the woman must not be lost, for to permit further erosion of the legal structure which protects women and which supports the family will surely sound the death knell for the family and society.

The achievement of excellence and high productive efficiency depends on the freedom for the individual and for those with organizational responsibility to be discriminating in their judgments and decisions. To recognize differences in people in no way violates our democratic principles. There are tasks only women can do best and certain ones men can do best. There is nothing wrong with the separation of the sexes under certain circumstances; not to separate them can spell disaster. Obviously not all men are equal in ability, nor are all women, nor are men and women equivalent. How society rewards differences in people is a complex issue. There is where injustice exists.

The simple truth is that even when socially conditioned to compete athletically with either sex, females nonetheless, if left alone, avoid contact sports. This is so because of the *biological* differences between male and female. Watch the play of a group of little girls and a group of little boys, and you can see immediately how different boys and girls are. The winning of war depends on raw, controlled vicious aggression and physical strength. Men, not women, will win wars, because they have more of these qualities.

The Women's Liberation movement has thrust women into areas of work where bonding and cooperation among men is essential to the most efficient and effective carrying out of a particular task or function. Male-male bonding is a socializing force which binds large numbers of men together in a common cause or purpose.[3] Examples range from social organizations to work forces of various kinds to the armed forces.

Placing women among men disrupts this bonding, the more so when the members are in close quarters for prolonged periods of time. This is so because the male-female bond is very powerful, and it is private, possessive and is jealously guarded. Men will not keep their presence nearly as well as when there are no women present.

The male is by nature protective of the female and all the more so when he loves a particular female. Men would unnecessarily expose themselves to the hazards of war in their efforts to protect the fighting women in their midst. I have had Viet Nam veterans tell me of their great horror when they discovered they had killed an enemy woman. The guilt eats away at them. Even though the woman was an enemy, killing her violated a powerful natural force within the male; namely, to protect the female. Anticipating the harm that might come to their female comrades would place the men in a constant state of added strain and cause them to disregard their own safety to some degree, and probably totally, at crucial moments.

That the men would be distracted because of their sexual attraction can be illustrated by two incidents: An Army woman in training with the men was injured and sent to the hospital. She received *forty* single roses from the men in her unit. A naval officer reported that during a landing exercise, he noticed that the *entire* group of men had their eyes trained on a woman who was at the tiller. He said, "As she was spinning the wheel around her fanny was oscillating back and forth; *all* my men had their eyes on her instead of attending to last minute preparations for landing. That is when I decided women do not belong in combat or aboard ship."[4]

Obviously the work force of society will mix the sexes to some degree—this is inevitable, necessary, and not all bad by any means. However, there are situations where the sexes should be kept separate. The feminists want women to have carte blanche access to all aspects of life. This is a mistake—just as it is a mistake for men to want to intrude totally into the woman's world.

There *are* tasks which men do better than women and vice versa. The most obvious basis for separating the sexes with regard to tasks to be performed is physical strength. The simple truth is that on the average, men are stronger than women. Women are about 60 percent as strong as men, and even if they are of equal weight, the woman is about 20 percent less powerful.

Forcing heavy industry to hire a certain quota of women is wrong. To do so will eventually lower the efficiency of the particular industry. While equal opportunity is a fine guiding concept, unequal ability (in this instance, based on physical strength) is a fact of life. This fact cannot be ignored, but the feminists insist that society ignore it, and they are having their way. The cost to society is enormous.

Women are taught to be competitive and hostile toward men. Competition in the business world, the market place, etc. is a fact of life, but within the bounds of the heterosexual relationship, and certainly within the family the sexes must be in harmony. The prevailing attitude of the moment is for women to square off against men, compete with them, point to them as exploiters who demean women. This philosophy inevitably carries over into the home. The sexes should make love, not war!

Sometimes a photograph or a visual image captures the essence of what is happening far better than a highly controlled (well-designed) research study. Look at a photo of various scenes of training at West Point. There you see those fine strong men performing well—and mixed among them are women—smaller in size, thinner arms, narrower shoulders, broad hips, and milder in appearance—trying desperately to emulate the hard masculine qualities of the men, but failing miserably to do so.

The solution on the broad social level is for the equal opportunity concept to remain in force, but for the government to keep hands off and permit managers and executives to have the freedom to hire the best suited person (regardless of sex, race, or religion) for the particular job. The term "best suited" will inevitably mean a person is not well-suited at times because of their sex. The American way of life emerged because we had the freedom to make choices, the freedom to find the place where we could perform best. To be discriminating in judgment is not to be discriminatory or prejudicial.

Some of the goals and values of the Women's Liberation movement are quite valid, realistic, and progressive. However, the tendency to place career objectives above the importance of the family must be strongly and openly opposed. They are doing mankind a grave disservice by inculcating young women with this belief. It is wrong for the leaders of this movement, many of whom are career women, to encourage these young women who have married and have children to reduce their level of responsibility to their family. In this respect the Women's Liberation movement poses a threat to the family. Many young women who might overcome their difficulties during early years as homemakers are provided an easy way out. The more militant leaders of this movement clearly downgrade the value of a career of homemaking. Instead, they would have women chase after the values of men and compete with them.

One single inescapable fact must be faced. If young women are to be increasingly drawn into the working world through a change in social values, then who will provide care for the children many of these women will have? Making a family and caring for children is a full-time career which only the most mature should attempt. Society will pay an extremely high price if the enormous importance of child care by parents in a home is downgraded or lost sight of. Ever increasing numbers of children will eventually swell the ranks of emotionally disturbed adults. It has been estimated that ten to thirty million children are in need of psychiatric help. Suicide has become the second leading cause of death in the young. Deprive the child of a happy home life and you deprive him of his mental health. If current trends which downgrade the expression of a woman's femininity within a family are prominent among the eroding forces—society as we know it now will end. A strong society comprises strong men and women. Strong individuals come from only one place—from solid families.

Some aspects of the Women's Liberation movement should be strongly opposed. For society to endorse their antifemininity, their antifamily values, and their competitiveness with men is sheer nonsense. But worse than that the movement places a stamp of acceptability or normality on what is, in fact, a manifestation of psychiatric illness—that is, a social value which reflects the personal illness of a group of individuals. Of even graver significance are the proclamations of major professional organizations to the effect that homosexuality is merely a preferred life-style rather than a serious form of psychopathology. Alcoholism, drug addiction, and any other class of psychiatric illness might as well be called preferences too.

America must wake up soon, or we will so cripple our social system that other nations will outperform us. My advice to men is to go out into the work force and compete against women just as if they were men. Do not be so chivalrous and gallant. Remember your job is at stake. To managers and executives my advice is to select the best person for the job, and if you are accused of being discriminatory against women, prove in court that you are not. Make your case, and put up a fight. You are basically fighting *for* your country. If a woman can do the task best, then hire her, of course. Where mixing the sexes lowers efficiency, then they should not be mixed; either hire all women or all men depending on the nature of the work to be done.

When men assert themselves in the work force, women who have intruded into areas where men function better will be forced out. They will then need jobs which they can do better than men, or equally as well. Furthermore, when men behave more assertively and responsibly, some women will be happy to return to the home, inflation permitting. If men would be men, more women would be women, and the solidity of the family would be reestablished. This in turn would improve childhood development, and these healthier children would ring out the destructive elements of the Womens Liberation movement.

The simple truth is that there are only so many jobs that pay a sufficiently high wage for a family man to provide for his family and himself. This man must outcompete all others so he gets his job, or society must give priority to the family man or single parent (of either sex).

Three conditions must be met for the family to survive: (1) The man and woman must both be emotionally healthy enough to be able to make a family; (2) Society must provide a sufficient number of positions which pay enough for married men to provide for their families; and (3) Society must upgrade the recognition of the couple who make a family, in particular the woman so that her sense of worth is reinforced by factors other than those from within her family, e.g., the joy of watching her children develop well, praise from her husband, and so forth.

It is imperative that society address the issue of women in the work force, find fulfilling and rewarding places for her there, but *not* at the expense of family life. Based on my observations of women for forty years, I believe society will be astounded by how willing they are to make the family their primary career if men will be responsible and give them the security to do so, *and* if society will recognize their enormous value. No finer expressions of generosity, patience, devotion, care, dedication, and many more fine human qualities can be found than those which are demonstrated by mature women who gave us our life, nurtured us, and launched us into society.

Chapter Ten

The "Normalization" of Homosexuality

I have already pointed out the lowered capacity of increasing numbers of people (as reflected in the divorce rate and other statistics) to make the heterosexual bond durable. This trend is entirely predictable in light of the severe disturbances within the family life of the developing young. The sexual drive is a fundamental element in human nature; so too is the need for closeness with other human beings. Homosexuals have these needs and drives too, but they are so filled with irrational fear and guilt having to do with intimacy with a member of the opposite sex that they turn to a member of the same sex for the gratification of their needs. Statistics suggest that homosexuality is increasing; its visibility certainly is. A spokesman for the homosexuals claims there are 25 million of them in the United States. Reputedly one-fourth of the residents of San Francisco are homosexual.

Dr. Abram Kardiner, a distinguished physician, psychoanalyst, and anthropologist, has stated that homosexuality reaches an epidemic level in societies which are in crisis or in a state of collapse.[1] The fact that homosexuals are coming "out of the closet" in droves, and are agitating for free access to all aspects of society is an ominous sign indeed. Even more ominous is the fact that a number of powerful mental health organizations have placed what amounts to a stamp of normality on this condition and have endorsed many of their social objectives.[2]

The increase in numbers of homosexuals and the increasing inclination of society to open all doors to them and even to define their psychological sickness as normal is one of the many manifestations of the disintegration of our society. Do not be fooled by homosexual propaganda which claims we are in an age of enlightenment, that the condition is merely a variation of normality.

I am frequently asked the question "What is wrong with permitting homosexuals to participate in all aspects of society and, further, who is to say their way of life is not normal? After all, haven't there always been homosexuals, including some very great people? And further, what difference does it make what people do in private?"

Before answering those questions, the true nature of the condition should first be discussed.

A fundamental question regarding human nature is whether man is biologically bisexual. Solid evidence strongly suggests he is not. Until about seven weeks, the human embryo is bipotential, but then events take place which cause the embryo to develop along existing lines and become female or change its direction and become male. To be sure, men and women have some common component parts, and common characteristics, but when the sum of the parts is added up, the "wholes" (male and female) are strikingly different. A child is born with enormous potential locked in his biology. Life experience unlocks this potential and develops it. None is more fundamental then that which leads to gender identity. Good parenting accomplishes this development.

Animals do not display true homosexual behavior. They do occasionally show displacement behavior, that is, they will at times mount (but not penetrate) a member of the same sex, but this does not occur when a sexually receptive female is available. Displacement behavior is nothing more than seeking out an object onto which to express a drive or impulse of motivation when the drive-specific object is not available. Homosexuals displace their sexual drives onto members of the same sex, *not* because of the unavailability of the opposite sex, but because *severe psychological conflicts* within their own minds prevent them from gratifying their sexual needs and need for interpersonal closeness with a member of the opposite sex to a completely satisfying degree.

Much publicity was recently given to apparent homosexuality among seagulls and naturally the gays and some professionals made much of this. Further study, however, showed that there was a shortage of the opposite sex among these gulls. Nature was compelling them to live out the mating instinct even though a suitable mate did not exist. Such animal behavior does not demonstrate fundamental homosexuality in man. Another study of ten thousand seagulls on Long Island failed to find a single incident of "homosexuality".[3] Quite predictably, an even number of male and female seagulls existed in this study.

If homosexuality reflected a fundamental bisexuality then it should appear in all cultures. It does not, and furthermore, its prevalence is much greater in highly advanced societies where family life suffers greater disturbances. The condition is unknown among the Ute and Apache Indians, in the aborigines, and in some tribes in Africa.

Hormonal studies do not correlate with the condition. Occasionally a report appears where the male hormone level is lower in the homosexual group (vs. heterosexual), but these reports are rare. Even if such reports were common, the field of psychosomatic medicine could easily explain the finding. We know that psychological conflicts and the emotions can have powerful effects on physiological processes, even on life itself. It would come as no surprise if homosexuals had lower male hormone levels, but most studies show they do not.

Twin studies do not exist where identical twins were separated at birth and reared by different parents, where these twins nonetheless *both* became homosexual. That there is greater homosexuality in identical twins in contrast to non-identical twins reared by the same parents proves nothing. The common pattern is for one child among several siblings to become homosexual. Since identical twins are generally the same, it follows logically that both should become homosexual.

It is very interesting to note that not all identical twins show a high concordance of homosexuality. More often, one of the twins is homosexual and the other is not.[4] When the family patterns are looked into, it has been found that the male homosexual member of the twin pair (these are male twins) was the mother's favorite while the heterosexual twin counterpart was emotionally closer to the father. These facts provide powerful additional support for the view that homosexuality is not caused by biological factors. This study is entirely consistent with the work of Beiber.[5]

Chromosomal studies do not reveal differences in heterosexuals and homosexuals, and it is highly unlikely that differences will appear in the molecular configuration of the genes (RNA and DNA). Even if differences should appear, such a finding could hardly place the stamp of normality on homosexuality. Some of man's most severe illnesses are caused by biological disturbances, cancer in particular. Sickle cell anemia is another example.

Finally, homosexuality is treatable by psychological methods when the treating person is knowledgeable about the human condition, is skilled in certain psychotherapeutic techniques, and *if* his own personality is free from certain personality disturbances. Obviously, a homosexual doctor would have difficulty helping a patient resolve the psychological conflicts which lead to his homosexuality because of the doctor's own psychological conflicts *and* his belief that homosexuality is normal.

Homosexuality is caused by the nature of the parents' interaction with the developing infant and child. This process is profoundly influenced by the personalities of both parents and the nature of their relationship with each other. The data which have been collected by doctors who do in-depth (psychoanalytic) studies of people for the purpose of helping them overcome their disturbance are entirely consistent with studies of the family patterns of homosexuals. The so-called "close binding" mother or the anxious or hostile mother and the absent or remote and hostile father causes the boy to never develop properly. Instead he develops severe emotional conflicts which prevent him from becoming a self-confident male who can experience loving and sexual feelings toward a woman. Little girls go through a comparable development; however, often their fathers were much too close to them. Excellent books and articles exist which describe the nature of this condition.[6]

My purpose in devoting a chapter to this condition is to suggest that the increase in the number of homosexuals and their aggressive social movement (the aim of which is to gain access to all aspects of society *and* to have their way of life defined as normal), is another and very ominous sign of the deterioration of our society. Their movement reflects a "normalization" of human qualities and a way of life which is one of the most severe disturbances of the human condition. The most obvious justification for that statement is the fact that *if* all people were homosexual the species would cease to exist. Furthermore, studies into the minds of homosexuals reveal the presence of profound conflicts which not only explain the condition, but lead indisputably to the definition of psychopathology. Now, to return to the questions asked earlier.

All cultures, including ancient Greece and Rome, have placed severe limitations on homosexual behavior when it existed in their culture. Biblical writers have done so also. The reason for this universal stance is obvious. To define the condition as normal permits a way of life to become part of the social fabric and to have a destructive feedback effect on individuals as well as social processes. Sick or destructive ways of behaving are prohibited or downgraded by customs, traditions, and laws in order to protect and stabilize society.

Today our own society is struggling with the issue of how far it will go in permitting homosexuals to permeate society, e.g., the classroom, the mental health profession, the armed forces, "marriage," etc. Obviously, homosexuals have a right to live in the society that created them. However, I do not believe they should be permitted to occupy any social position of their choice.

This same principle applies to all individuals. There are places where we fit or belong and can contribute to society in a constructive manner and there are places where we cannot; this fact is obvious. The issue of homosexuals in the classroom as teachers is a hot issue currently. If the premise is accepted that children on up through junior high level and even high school level should be exposed to the most healthy (emotionally) individuals possible, then homosexuals should be excluded from the teaching profession at least to the high school level. Obviously, many emotionally disturbed heterosexuals should be excluded as well. Young children should be exposed to the healthiest adults possible. For some children their school teacher is the healthiest person who will have an impact on their developing personalities.

The homosexuals are making a grave mistake by attempting to "sell" society on the notion that theirs is a normal condition, or one that is freely chosen and that they should have free access to all aspects of society. They would, in the long run, be far less ostracized, and perhaps not at all, if they admitted they are emotionally disturbed, asked society to show compassion for them, and assimilate them into society where their sickness would not adversely affect the young or emotionally vulnerable. What appears to be discrimination against homosexuals is society's way of insuring itself against the feedback and destructive impact of a sick condition which disturbs family life.

Homosexuals are emotionally sick people. If a society incorporates this way of life into its basic structure, it too becomes a sicker society and therefore and inevitably a weakened one. Since gender identity; that is, what defines a male and female, is at the very heart of the cultural revolution which is sweeping through our nation, it is imperative that strong and healthy people take a stand against the gay propagandists. It is equally imperative for vulnerable heterosexuals to not be tipped into the homosexual world for their own personal welfare and for the best interests of society.

If you learn that your son or daughter is homosexual, you should face it squarely. Do not panic, and above all, do not reject your child. To do so will almost surely consolidate the homosexual condition. Many who are homosexual will simply flatly refuse offers of help, but make the offer nonetheless. Try to find a professional person who is expert in this area of psychopathology and obtain help for your child. Do not give up if you don't find help immediately. Our society sorely needs treatment centers for homosexuals, but until the day arrives when such centers exist, individuals will have to seek help on their own through private sources. Help does exist, not enough to treat all, but some at least. The most enlightened and determined individuals will be able to find that help.

To ignore your child's homosexuality, or to try to convince yourself that the condition is normal is nothing more than a way to deny your part in his emotional development, and of course, this is the strategy of the gay community; call the condition normal, so they do not have to do anything about it.

Chapter Eleven

Pornography: A Barometer of the Nation's Sickness

Pornography in its various forms is a multibillion dollar business in the United States, depicting all of the perversions, and it debases women in the worst possible way. This business flourishes because of its appeal to millions of Americans. The simple curiosity of emotionally healthy people would never support the ever-expanding pornography industry. This business is a shocking and ominous barometer of the state of emotional health of millions of our fellow citizens. It confirms the institutionalization of psychopathology. Worse, our laws and lawmakers, whose function and duty it is to maintain the best values of society, are slowly but surely yielding to the impact of the ever-increasing mass of sickness which has found expression in this particular form. The federal courts' application of the principle of community standards with regard to what is obscene, beautifully illustrates how human psychopathology eventually permeates the values of society—in this instance with the blessing of the courts.

In addition to outright pornography, the open display of near-explicit sex appears everywhere. It is difficult to watch television without observing outright sex and, of course, violence too. There appear to be as many

"R" rated movies as those rated suitable for the young.
Our society has relaxed its constraint on sexuality so
extensively that the senses are dulled to these stimuli.
However, the consequences for society are profound. Illegitimate births are soaring and pregnancy among teen-
agers is at an epidemic level. The consequences of all of
this are downright tragic. Sex has become a part of even
the most casual relationships.

Less obvious but equally serious is the overall lower-
ing of cultural excellence within our country. It has been
repeatedly observed that there is an inverse relationship between sexual license and the cultural excellence.
That is to say, the sexual drive is a force within the
creative process. When most of the sexual energy of a
society is expressed directly as raw sex, less of its energy finds its way into the creative process.

Sexual expression between mature couples who have
a meaningful relationship adds depth to life. One can
dine well or degenerate into gluttony. The same applies
to sex. When the social pattern tilts toward sexual gluttony, the culture will trend toward decline. This is happening in our country.

The unbridled sexual expression of today and the
flourishing pornography business are a direct outgrowth
of the breakdown of family life. I will describe this relationship in this chapter, and thereby demonstrate again
how very sick our society has become. It is inevitable
that broken, strained, or part-time families will lead to
disturbed personality development and that those disturbances will lead to a breakdown of rational constraints
on sexuality, to rampant pornography, and to an overall
cultural decline.

In order to best understand the origin of pornography and how pornography in turn influences the individual and society, it is necessary to explain the appeal
of pornography, that is, to explain what it is in people
that makes them produce and view such material, and
how their actions stem from disturbed family life.

The strength and permanence of the heterosexual
bond, the commitment between a man and a woman

within the institution of the family, directly determines the outcome of the psychological development of the children they produce. In order for a man and woman to attain a high level of commitment, their own personalities must be relatively free from emotional conflicts and psychopathology. The more complete the sense of maleness and femaleness the couple has achieved, the more harmonious their relationship will be. The healthiest children are produced by mature, masculine men and mature, feminine women who deeply love each other and whose family life has not been disrupted by the cruel hand of fate.

An outright broken home places a severe handicap on the child. These conflicts cannot be resolved when one parent is gone. A weak father who is jealous of his son drives the boy ever closer to his mother, rather than drawing the son closer to him, and out of the romantic tie with his mother. Fathers often are much too close to their daughters. Some parents are outright seductive toward the child of the opposite sex, but are unaware of being so. Volumes have been written about these human developmental processes and their consequences. *The disturbances of childhood development provide the basis for an interest in pornography.*

Pornography depicts all of the perversions, including homosexuality, and often in its rawest form. Lacking in all of the depictions of heterosexual intercourse, regardless of style or form, is even the remotest reference to love between the man and woman. It is raw sex, usually highly perverse, and nothing else. Bowel and bladder functions are included in pornographic material and, more recently, children and animals are included in pornographic movies, pictures, and writings. Sadism and masochism, that is, the aggressive instinct, is also part of the pornographic scene. More recently, the theme of incest, usually between father and daughter, is depicted or alluded to.

A perversion is nothing more than the substitution of another mode for expressing sexual instinct rather than the genital one, or the substitution of the normal

object (a member of the opposite sex) with someone or
something else onto which the sexual impulse is to be
released, or both. Perverse sexual behavior may show
disturbance in mode and object of sexual expression.
The reasons for these substitutions include those developmental fixations or arrests, to which I referred earlier, and the severe guilt and anxiety associated with
childhood genital sexuality which was never extinguished.
The guilt and anxiety force the sexual instinct to find
expression in some way other than the genital route
with a member of the opposite sex. Or, if sexual expression can take that route, it is dehumanized, nearly always degrades the woman, and is devoid of any expression of love between the participants.

Homosexuality is one of the consequences of serious
childhood disturbances in psychosexual development.
This is an abnormal condition, and as could be expected,
homosexual X-rated movies are part of the pornographic
scene. When society sanctions the distribution of pornographic material, it is legitimizing (normalizing) psychopathology.

The fact that pornography or nearly explicit sex is
displayed on the screen, on the printed page, and even
on television, practically without restraint, is a sign of
the decay of our society. The few successful prosecutions
of the perpetrators of pornography are pitiful indeed.
These few successes are virtually meaningless in the
face of the tidal wave of the billions of dollars of profit
which are made through the distribution of pornography. In order for these billions to be made, millions of
Americans enjoy looking at it. What does this say about
the American character?

It says just exactly what you are thinking. Increasing numbers of Americans contain substantial psychopathology within themselves and do not reach full maturity. They cannot find fulfillment in their personal lives
generally and with a member of the opposite sex in particular. Instead they find gratification through pornography, or free-wheeling sexual behavior. The simple truth
is that mature men and women have no interest in por-

nography and promiscuous sexuality. Their curiosity may
lead to an inspection of pornography, but they do not
generate a persistent interest in it. They do not simply
because there is little in their unconscious minds to which
the material can appeal. They would rather experience
sex *and love* with and for their spouse, because that is
where their maturity takes them. While another barometer is hardly needed as regards the trend our society is
taking, the wide appeal of pornography tells us very
clearly what is happening to the psychological health of
millions of us and to the value system in which we live.
Perverse sex and sex without love and commitment is
part of the times. Unless this growing trend is reversed,
and until the heterosexual bond is strong once again for
a larger proportion of Americans, we will continue on
our downward slide and may eventually see the end of
the America which once led the world in almost all respects. Depraved sexuality and epidemic homosexuality
are signs of a dying culture. Recall what happened in
ancient Rome.

While individuals contribute to the form taken by
society, society also affects the individual. In other words,
while the pornography industry is the outgrowth of individual psychopathology, the industry itself has a feedback effect on individuals. How then does pornography
affect people? There are several ways:

1. The very healthy may, out of curiosity, view the
material; they may even experiment a bit in their personal lives with what they saw, but soon discard it all.

2. Older people whose sexual powers are declining
may erroneously believe viewing pornographic material
will improve their sex lives. While their excitement may
be temporarily heightened, their performance will not
be. More often they will not be able to equal the "performance" of those they viewed or read about, and will end
up with even lower self-esteem than before. Their own
performance anxiety will be heightened and their performance impaired.

3. Believing they are keeping in step with the times,
a couple may introduce some of the behavior—usually

clearly perverse—into their sexual pattern with each other. While it may be true that "variety is the spice of life," this phrase does not apply to the variations of the sexual theme as depicted by pornography. Couples may severely offend each other through the introduction of the perversions to their sex life. A man may grow dissatisfied with his wife on the erroneous belief that just because she does not go through all the gyrations he saw on the screen, she is dull. His wife may, in fact, be capable of the deepest of feeling for him and capable of fine orgasmic response. What more could any reasonable man want? Couples are being misguided and misinformed as to what is best in man-woman relations through pornography, and have divorced because of the man's growing discontent with his wife because of his continual exposure to X-rated movies.

4. Young people who would otherwise work out a satisfactory and mature sexual style after they marry, nowadays carry with them a repertoire of techniques which they learned from viewing X-rated movies. In times past, and because their psychosexual development was reasonably good, they would have adhered to a more mature standard of behavior, i.e., heterosexual intercourse. Now, having been exposed to pornography, they more often try out other forms of sexual activity. To do so runs the risk of introducing immature and perverse sexual behavior into their sexual pattern and thereby induces a psychological regression. I will illustrate this with a case history further on.

5. Society is filled with increasing numbers of people who, because of their emotional conflicts, are extremely vulnerable to the effects of pornography. This is so because they come from disturbed or broken families. Their unconscious minds are filled with the conflicts I described earlier. Viewing pornographic material triggers these elements and induces less mature behavior. Once these unconscious forces have been integrated into overt behavioral patterns it is very difficult to remove them. This category of people I believe accounts for the fact that pornography has become a multibillion dollar-a-year industry.

A case illustration will demonstrate the conflict triggering effects of pornography on a vulnerable young man. The effects of his behavior on his new bride were profound and produced extreme changes in her personality, and nearly wrecked their marriage. In high school this young fellow appeared to be the all-American boy. He was a good student, and athlete, and he had high aspirations for the future. His family life had not been the best, however, and certain developmental disturbances were the result. On balance the healthy side of him outweighed the sick elements. In college, he began to date and promptly developed anxiety in association with his efforts to be close to his girl friends. For reasons he could not at first explain, he was drawn to X-rated movies and various pornographic publications, probably to reassure himself by feeling more familiar with sex. He soon became preoccupied with this exposure. He was attempting to overcome his anxieties about heterosexual intimacy. Not only did the movies and publications *not* help him, he picked up ideas that he had never thought of or heard of. Before long he initiated these various sexual techniques with women, avoiding frank intercourse. Eventually he managed to have intercourse, provided the young woman emulated prostitute-type behavior.

Within a few years he met a fine young woman who appealed to the healthy elements in him. They were married within a year. She entered marriage with high expectations. Her highest dream was to have a family. She was a feminine young woman who approached her wedding night fully expecting to be loved by her manly-appearing husband. She was bitterly disappointed. Within a few weeks after marriage this man began criticizing her values. He deprecated her frilly nighty. He wanted her to wear black things and garters. He performed the well-known perversions with her, including anal intercourse. She felt cheapened, degraded, and became non-orgasmic. Her feelings became totally inhibited when it became apparent that her husband felt no love whatsoever for her during his sexual activities with her.

This woman soon developed an interest in feminist literature and eventually became an ardent and militant member of that movement. Life had taught her that women *are* only sexual objects and instruments for the depraved behavior of men. This couple eventually found their way into psychiatric treatment where both made substantial changes for the better. They eventually overcame their unconscious conflicts, and the healthy aspects which had held them together grew and flourished. They eventually created a family.

The woman was astounded by the discovery in her treatment that she too had marked psychosexual disturbances within the depths of her. These had contributed to her choice of this man, even though she failed at the time to recognize this fact. Had her husband been a totally healthy, or even a healthier man, his impact on her would have been entirely different. She would not have undergone the psychological regression and, in all likelihood, she would have matured in response to him and would have never required psychiatric help. Instead, his interest in pornography and her exposure to it induced a profound regression and a revision of her entire value system.

Had this young man not been introduced to sexual perversions and sex through pornography, his chances of maturing within the context of his marriage would have increased. The bond between the healthy elements in both of them would have induced further maturation in both through mutual reinforcement.

Common sense tells us pornography influences the individual. My own clinical experience convinces me without any doubt. A few studies provide further support to this belief. The surgeon general's report of 1972 shows an unmistakable link between TV violence and violent behavior in children. The Bartells' book on group sex states that couples who entered into this type of behavior attribute the onset of their behavior to pornography.[1] The article by Malamultz and Fishback states their belief that viewing pornography lifts not only the taboo on sex, but also the taboo on aggression. They believe that "viewing the erotic film, we communicate the unspoken message that taboo behavior like sex is O.K.;" "men exposed to violent pornography were more sexually aroused than others by reading the story of a rape;" and "psychologists, in our opinion, ought not support, implicitly or explicitly, the use of violent pornography."

It was inevitable that the disturbed psychosexual development of the millions of children who grew up, and continue to grow up, in less than good family circumstances, would eventually find expression in the social scene in a raw and undisguised form. The flourishing pornography business is that expression. Pornography depicts on the screen, the printed page, on television, and on the live stage, what exists in the sick personalities of millions of our fellow Americans.

When responsible adults permit this sickness to be displayed virtually without any restriction, the younger members of society believe that elders condone these forms of behavior. New values are thereby introduced into society. Abnormal sexuality which is depicted in pornographic material, and mature sexuality should, in my opinion, be recorded in two places only—in medical textbooks and other scientific papers, and in true literary creations where a point is to be made about the human condition. Society and individuals alike can only be harmed when we "legitimize" psychopathology and fail to place reasonable restraints on sexuality in general. For a society to survive, it must strengthen the constructive elements within it and within people. It is the responsibility of the state, the church, and the family to continually address this issue.

Chapter Twelve

Can America Survive? A Call to Arms

The vitality of a nation is the sum of the vitality of its people. The vitality of a nation is reflected in its productive efficiency, its creativeness in all aspect of life, ranging across the spectrum from the sciences to the humanities and the arts. A nation's vitality is also reflected in its values, traditions, laws, and social mores. America has ranked at the top in nearly all aspects of this definition of a vital nation. The free world has relied upon us for leadership and protection.

In order for individual vitality to be able to contribute to national vitality each individual must have the freedom to develop his potential and express it in the society which created him. Too rigid a social structure enslaves the human spirit and fails to evoke and develop human potential. Tradition stabilizes a society but societies that are too tradition-bound do not keep pace with the social progress enjoyed by freer societies.

In America we have produced very vital and strong individuals. These individuals have been able to find the opportunities to express their abilities, and as a consequence ours has been a very vigorous nation. We enjoy enormous freedom, and our society permits social change to occur. It is imperative that social change be construc-

tive. While the United States is still the source of strength
for the stability of the world, serious doubt is being
expressed by many thoughtful individuals within our
own nation, and from nations whose security depends on
us, whether we possess the national will to carry on in
this leadership and protective capacity.

The United States Treasury, at one time, seemed
inexhaustible. We have financed the rebuilding of the
nations we destroyed in war. We have sponsored the
growth of underdeveloped nations. Our national debt
has grown steadily as those in charge lacked the vision
or courage and strength required to place restraint on
policies which created the huge national debt. For the
first time in history, our government no longer borrows
just from its own people, but is borrowing money from
foreign countries as well. This trend reflects a serious
weakness in the leadership of America and in the national will.

Equally ominous is the lowered productive efficiency
of the other industrialized nations which is increasing
while ours is decreasing. The United States is now ranked
the lowest in productive efficiency among the industrialized nations of the West. Great worry exists among our
national leaders about our lag in technological innova-
tion.

While the balance of trade deficit is in part attribut-
able to oil imports, this factor by no means accounts for
all of the deficit. Japan has no oil whatsoever yet has a
huge trade surplus. Their productive efficiency is increasing while ours is dropping. Their people work harder
and more efficiently. The family unit is very solid in
Japan, perhaps as strong as anywhere else in the world.

Predictably the value of the dollar has dropped at
home and abroad despite its recent strength brought
about by high interest rates. This decline in part reflects
the opinion other nations have of the American character and its will. Our leaders have debased the dollar.
Leaders with an iron will who can manage finances wisely,
who do not overspend, no longer seem to exist. No leader
seems to exist who has the courage to say *No* to the

insatiable demands of virtually every sector of society. Instead, the printing press rolls on and on, and inflation will spiral ever upward despite a temporary decline.

While high interest rates have temporarily strengthened the dollar, the consequences are high unemployment and serious recession, if not outright depression. It is but a matter of time before the weakened will of our leaders manifests itself and we reinflate again. Federal deficits have *never* permanently diminished. What is happening to America?

The answer to that question is not difficult to find. *Americans* have changed and are continuing to change. As they change, social values change. Currently the direction of that change is toward disintegration and weakness rather than strength. The present day leadership of America was put there by a changed people. The key question is whether a sufficient number of strong Americans exist so as to be able to outvote the weak Americans who have placed weak leaders in power. A strong president can be completely crippled by a Congress which gives in to the will of the people, who want to *get* from their country, rather than *give* to it.

In view of the fact that the divorce rate continues to climb—it is now 50 percent—and that approximately one-half of our young people are spending a major portion of their developmental years in living arrangements other than true families, our future is uncertain at best. This is so because all of those personality factors; the confluence of which lead to strength of character, strength of will, capacity for commitment, the ability to work hard, and the quest for excellence—will be diminished to some degree in millions of young people whose responsibility it will be to carry our society forward.

These millions of individuals will inevitably select leaders for government who will promise to give to them rather than expect to get from them. A child who has been deprived during his early developmental years lives his life wanting to get from others; he continually attempts to fill himself up in one way or another. By contrast, those who have received abundant emotional input from their parents during their developmental years, are full of life and go out into the world with the capacity to give to life, and make society move forward. Multiply this formula by the millions of children who have missed out on bountiful home life, and it provides a clearer picture of why it is probable that the public will place weak leaders in office who will give them what they want and thereby ever increase the size of the national debt.

As the national debt grows, inflation will re-ignite and more women will be forced out of the home and into the work place. Their babies and small children will be more deprived than filled. When they grow up, they will trend toward wanting to *take from* rather than *contribute to* society. They will join the swelling ranks of those who elect leaders who will give them what they want, ever increasing the size of the national debt and so on and on until the currency becomes worthless, and the economy collapses. We are already well on our way. Despite our president's very sincere wish to reduce the size of the federal debt, he is failing. The voice of those who want nurture is too loud. Granted, there are truly needy people, and the governmental steps to reverse inflation have caused many to become unemployed through no weakness of character of their own; yet, there are too many in government who lack the strength of character to stand firm and correct the economic ills.

Other nations always know when a nation is becoming weak. The international scene is a dog-eat-dog world; nations always exist which will quickly fill a vacuum.

America is a compassionate nation, but the massive immigration into our country is cause for deep concern. The flagrant way Castro dumped his "undesirables" on us was successful because our administration was too weak to prevent this shocking event from occurring. People made the decision to let them in. Look at their strength of character, and you will see weakness and passivity behind the facade of compassion. Rome was eventually invaded, and so are we being invaded because we have become too weak to erect and enforce immigration barriers.

Many who do immigrate will undoubtedly embrace the solid values of America and contribute to her strength, but vast numbers will not. There has not been sufficient time for them to thoroughly accommodate to our values. Generally, the strongest supporters of any nation's values are those who are born in that nation, grow up in a solid family, and adapt to that nation's values from childhood onward.

This is no time to "hope for the best," to assume that our situation will somehow turn itself around. We—all of us—have the responsibility to turn it around. I believe each of us has a dual responsibility. First, we must try to develop our own potential to the fullest and thereby become able to make our contributions to life. Secondly, we must take a greater interest in our nation and try to save it. Each person will find his own way to do that; however, I have a few suggestions toward these objectives. We simply *must* take care of our beloved America.

Do not marry until you feel ready for it, and after you do marry, spare no effort to make your marriage succeed. A successful marriage will do more for you personally, for your children *and* for society than anything I can think of. As I have said repeatedly, the family— the healthy family—is the building block of any society; the main key to civilization; it is the pivotal point around which all else turns. However, do not assume the worst about your marriage. Many couples survive the inevitable rough waters of the early days of marriage and both parties grow emotionally as they work out their marital difficulties. It is always easier to run away from a problem than to persist and eventually solve it. The latter course nearly always brings greater rewards.

When marital strife begins, the grass always looks greener elsewhere, but it frequently is not. Give yourselves time to mature and resolve your problems. The trauma of divorce, to yourselves and to your children, is great. Spare no effort to make your marriage work.

Look squarely at how you live your personal life. Do the values you live by help or hurt you and our society? It is every person's responsibility to treat well the great gift of life. Not only will you be doing yourself a service, but you will be serving your country in this way. The writer of the Ten Commandments understood life; live by those principles. They have been tested by time and experience; live by them. In other words, re-examine the ethical system you live by and strengthen the weak spots.

Examine the social scene, and in particular, that of which you are a part. Ask yourself, "What can I do for my country that I am not now doing?" There is plenty you can do, and we had better take better care of our country, or we will lose her, if not now, almost certainly for our children and future generations. Align yourself with a social cause that interests you, but before you do, check it out very carefully, and be certain its net effect is a constructive one.

Organizations of all kinds exist and are springing up continually which are sponsored by citizen groups. Look into these and join forces with them. There are coalitions for decency, there are anti-pornography groups, anti-drug groups, all appearing throughout the land. Parents are banding together for the purpose of examining school books for the purpose of identifying those which advocate untested new life-styles for the young. Groups have formed to counteract the poisonous propaganda that "gay is good"—that is, that homosexuality is a normal life-style. Use your great gift of intelligence and think about the social decay which is upon us, and find an organization that is trying to do something about it, and join up, or create one of your own.

Of particular importance are legislative watchdog groups. New social values sooner or later become social norms. Some, of course, are constructive, but many are not. Someone inevitably wants to get these values written into law, and new laws do get written; some are good and some are not. The effort to "decriminalize" the use of marijuana is an example of how social values eventually influence the laws. The Women's Liberation movement's effort to change the law with regard to permitting women to enter the combat areas of the armed forces is another. Bussing schoolchildren away from their neighborhood schools is sheer madness. While the intent behind bussing was good, the effects are disastrous. The experiment simply hasn't worked, yet this monstrous injustice to our children continues.

Just as stability in the home is necessary for child development so too is stability in the school. The family, the school, and the church all provide those human experiences which lead to strength of personality. Bussing children across town breaks up the sense of continuity that is so necessary in a child's life. Parents cannot participate as well in school functions. The child lives in two worlds; one at home and the other way off somewhere at school. The sense of involvement cannot develop in the child when he is shipped away from his "home" territory.

Before you vote anyone into office, look into their personal lives and *look at their personality*. What a man or woman *is* determines to a large extent what he *believes*. I look very closely at the personalities and backgrounds of people who find their way into public office. Professional ethics prevents me from revealing what is glaringly obvious to me about some of our leaders who are in key positions of leadership and about some who are seeking office. You have to have a very healthy personality and a very strong will to be able to live by our best values, and when in office uphold them and stand up to other national leaders, and say "You will not cross this line." Far too many of our leaders and lawmakers lack this strength.

I do not believe our situation is hopeless, but it is one nonetheless which requires *everyone* to wake up and take stock. Put your life in the most constructive direction possible. Save your family, be the best parent you can possibly be, and then start looking after your country. America needs all of us like she has never needed our help before. If she does not receive this help soon, our way of life, and indeed our nation will almost surely cease to exist within a generation or two—or sooner. The future is in *our* hands and my message to you is a call to arms!

Appendix One

Psychotherapy

I will now discuss various types of psychiatric treatment, with special emphasis being placed on the psychotherapeutic process.

Psychotherapy refers to all forms of treatment which rely on interpersonal interactions, including psychoanalysis. It can do much good or it can do great harm. The results of treatment depend upon the personality of the person doing the treating, his grasp of the nature of mental life and human existence, and treatment techniques. Also of immense importance are the life circumstances of the patient, the nature of the patient's problems, and his basic personality organization.

Those of you who need or who are in treatment may require help to determine whether you are being treated effectively or are being harmed. An understanding of what is written here will also be of help to those who never enter formal treatment, particularly those of you who are trying to help yourselves.

I will now focus on those principles which make psychotherapy successful. Psychotherapy is most effective when the physician takes responsibility for inducing change in his patient. This may seem to you like a perfectly obvious and necessary orientation to the treatment process, but it is not a guiding principle for many who practice psychotherapy.

It is around this point that I feel most critical toward so

many psychotherapists. Most seem to want sincerely to help their patients but they do not fully grasp the absolutely vital importance of taking responsibility for the patient and his treatment. The implications of this principle are far-reaching as I will illustrate. So many psychotherapists leave the responsibility of changing to the patient, failing to realize, apparently, that had the patient been able to change he would never have come to them in the first place.

During the treatment process, the doctor's responsibilities to his patient are: (1) he must induce change in his patient. To do this wisely and effectively the doctor must understand the human condition and he must have mastered techniques for bringing about constructive changes in his patient. (2) He must protect the patient from the irrational forces within himself which are unleashed during the treatment process. (3) He must protect others from these same forces within his patient. (4) He must help the patient develop his potentials and find ways for their expression.

Effective psychotherapy depends upon the patient's cooperation, of course, but bringing about change is the doctor's responsibility. As patients change (that is, resolve their unconscious conflicts and get over their symptoms and change their personality and behavior), responsibility gradually shifts from doctor to patient. By the end of treatment the patient becomes truly independent and can take full responsibility for himself, and that is as it should be. But even to the very last day of treatment the guiding orientation for the doctor should be one of responsibility. I believe psychotherapists should take responsibility for their patient twenty-four hours a day, seven days a week, just as other physicians do, and not limit their responsibility to the period of time when doctor and patient are meeting. The specifics of this guiding principle will be explained and illustrated as the treatment process is described. Meeting with a patient a specified number of times per week is a matter of practical convenience. The therapeutic process is set in motion at the outset of treatment and goes on continuously. Hence the doctor's responsibility is continuous; many doctors do not understand this fundamental point, at least they seem not to.

Many doctors do not fully understand the powerful impact they may be having on their patient or, conversely, how little; nor do they understand the power of the forces in the patient's unconscious mind which the treatment process releases. In either case, the element of the doctor's responsibility is a crucial factor in the proper conduct and outcome of the treatment.

Patients who have been effectively treated are able to enjoy life more. They are able to play more effectively; they tend to work less compulsively but at the same time they work more efficiently. Self-destructive tendencies disappear. Where a heterosexual relationship was impossible previously, it now becomes possible. Parenthood is possible. Creative talents become freed. Behavior that was once compulsive and stereotyped gives way to a more flexible, appropriate type of behavior. Work inhibitions disappear. Frank psychiatric symptoms disappear. Free-floating anxiety and depressive feelings, episodic or constant, should disappear. Sexual pleasure should increase.

A patient who has been thoroughly treated should have overcome identity difficulties. This refers to what he is in a vocational sense and also, and especially so, in the sense of gender. The effeminate man or masculine woman can be one of the most difficult kinds of patients to treat, but unless these mixed identities are changed, treatment was not totally successful. Naturally, persistent homosexuality after treatment has been terminated as a sure sign that treatment was a failure. The treatment may have helped the patient in some respects but failed in its most significant feature.

The success or failure of treatment can also be defined in terms of the original goals. If they have been reached it is probably legitimate to say that treatment was successful. The difficulty with this is that as treatment proceeds new psychopathology is inevitably uncovered. Original treatment goals are accordingly modified.

Many attitudes, values, character traits, behaviors, and even symptoms, will not yield to exploratory psychotherapy, including psychoanalysis. I think the reason for this is not so much that "uncovering" therapy is worthless but is due largely to the doctor's failure to realize that he must do more than bring insight to the patient.

I find it most distressing to hear of people who were in psychoanalysis many years but who are really no different afterwards. No doubt they discovered much about themselves but for all practical purposes they remained unchanged. Often patients have changed to some extent but not nearly enough to justify the high expenditure of time, money, and effort.

A successfully treated person should be able to do a great many things he could not do before treatment. Above all, he should be successful in his work, and should be able to marry and become a parent. He should, in short, be able to fulfill the definition of a normal man or woman.

What is it, then, that doctors do wrong? I am referring to therapists and analysts who strive to bring about extensive personality change but fail to do so. I think there are several things. They remain too detached, aloof, or neutral. Some even claim to be indifferent to the outcome of treatment. This is absolutely incredible to me. How can a physician remain neutral in the face of illness? Actually it is impossible to be neutral toward one's patient. Even in psychoanalysis, where such a stance is said to be necessary for the proper development of transference, the analyst cannot be neutral. Whenever he points something out to a patient, confronts him, makes an interpretation, he has abandoned neutrality. Nonetheless, I think Freud's cautioning that the analyst should not moralize, but should serve as a screen or mirror, has been over-done. Experience has shown that patients develop transference toward the doctor and others in their lives when there is no semblance of neutrality in the other persons.

I believe neutrality in the conduct of psychotherapy should be abandoned and the doctor should, as I noted earlier, take a stand for health and against illness. A patient needs to know where his doctor stands.

It is a complete myth that a psychotherapist can remain neutral toward his patient or in relation to what the patient tells about himself, his life, etc. Persons who attempt to remain neutral toward their patient are either fooling themselves or they are denying their patient one of the most effective aspects of treatment, or both. The doctor must be *accepting* of the patient but *rejecting* in relation to the patient's psychopathology, regardless of its form. At first this distinction is difficult for the patient to grasp inasmuch as he usually feels that his psychopathology is an integral part of himself, especially character traits and behavioral patterns of long standing. It rarely serves a purpose for the doctor to scold a patient for behaving in a certain way; however, even this extreme form of a stand against the patient's illness may be very effective and even necessary in some instances.

The principle here is that the doctor should ally himself with the mature and healthy aspects of his patient and that the two of them (doctor and the healthy part of the patient) align themselves against the patient's illness. There should be, then, a constant pressure in the therapeutic experience—the doctor's stand against illness and for health. Naturally this pressure or alignment alone will not cure the patient, but this clear orientation is, I believe, vital to treatment; it provides an outside force on the patient to change.

This point may seem self-evident to the lay public whose doctors openly take such a position against their physical illnesses. This attitude toward illness is not as pervasive among psychiatrists and psychoanalysts, and certainly not so among many of the varied persons who claim to be psychotherapists. In fact, some claim only to seek to provide understanding for the patient but will go no further than that. Some therapists form opinions (judgments) about the patient's behavior but keep them strictly to themselves, conveying an attitude of neutral interest to the patient. Some therapists are so disturbed in their own personalities and values that they openly reinforce the patient's illness. These stances deprive the therapist of valuable leverage. Some therapists and analysts believe it is their mission to help a patient go where he wants to go and be what he wants to be regardless of whether or not that behavior or way of being is pathological. I recall a psychoanalyst telling me he helped a young patient discover her homosexual inclinations and eventually settle into an overt homosexual way of life. This, in my opinion, is a total treatment failure.

The psychotherapist should always try to help the patient fulfill himself in life—fully develop his potentials and find suitable outlets for them—but fulfillment should come in a mature way. Unfortunately, the sick side of people seeks expression and fulfillment too. To foster this is to make sick people sicker. Many therapists help patients find greater peace of mind by helping them alter the environment to suit their personalities and needs, even though these include sick elements, rather than changing the patient's personality so it will fit better with the demands of the adult world. Patients have an uncanny way of selecting doctors who will be of little real help to them and who will reinforce their sickness. Psychotherapists should never just "help patients go where they want to go" unless it is clear that where they want to go is in a healthy direction. The exception is the very sick patient who cannot change and a place has to be found for him which provokes as little psychic disorganization as possible.

The essential point in the preceding remarks is that effective psychotherapy cannot be done without a value system by which the therapist is guided. No physician could practice physical medicine without values (urinalysis, blood analyses, chemical analyses, physical symptoms and signs, etc.) to guide him, to help him distinguish abnormality from normality, nor can a psychotherapist. Some may not realize this, but all are guided by a values system of some kind.

Therefore, an integral part of good treatment is the upholding of normal values. Within the range of normal there is ample room for diversity and individuality, for uniqueness. However, some ways of thinking, feeling, and behaving are clearly abnormal. Students of the human condition know this very well, and this knowledge must be used as a guide if one person is going to treat another effectively.

As treatment proceeds, the doctor first identifies the various forms of the patient's pathology and then attempts to discover the underlying reason for them. This process amounts to an appeal to the rational forces and strengths within the patient to abandon his illness, to grow. This has been discussed to some extent; however, to recapitulate, the doctor analyzes the patient's dreams, free associations, metaphors, slips, and transferences, and thereby exposes the underlying motivations for the pathology. However, it frequently develops that these insights do not cause the psychopathology to disappear.

Many dynamically oriented therapists rework the old insight, hoping that the next time around the problem will clear up. They also search in new directions on the assumption that there are other motivations yet to be discovered which, when found, will make possible the resolution of the patient's illness. The search continues, and sometimes this approach works but many times the search goes on for years, the insights get worked over again and again and grow stale, and the patient fails to change. Then what?

Some therapists and analysts rationalize their way out of such situations, thereby ducking their responsibility to the patient, by saying the patient now has all the insight there is to be found; and if he *wanted to* he would change, that to change is now a matter of free choice. I believe this is incorrect. Patients would change if they could.

I believe in the importance of insight; I always start treatment by searching out meanings behind the various forms of the patient's psychopathology. However, when insight fails to bring about change I think pressure should be applied on the patient. Pressure can take several forms. The most logical form of pressure to apply is encouragement; logical because most patients are lacking to some degree in the most essential human quality—courage. Patients should be encouraged to think more maturely, to behave in new and more mature ways; ways which suit the basic fabric of the patient's personality. At the same time, patients should be encouraged to abandon their old pathological ways. For example, a man should be actively advised and encouraged to stop treating his wife in immature, hostile, or provocative ways and, in turn, substitute better ways. He should be encouraged to abstain from immature or perverse sexual practices, and so on. A value system should be upheld to him and urged upon him; for instance, taking his place as the head of the family.

This combined pressure on the patient to abstain from the old sick ways on the one hand, and to behave in new and more mature ways on the other, will serve another very useful purpose besides helping him behave more maturely. It will also cause the patient's unconscious mind to pour out its contents. The reason for this is perfectly clear; since the old ways of thinking and behaving are blocked, the unconscious motivations must seek expression in some other way; they will surface somewhere since it is in the nature of things for unconscious forces to find expression, be it in symptoms, behavior, character style, dreams, or language. Furthermore, new ways of behaving will trigger those unconscious conflicts which prevented the patient from behaving maturely in the first place. The patient may begin to experience very intense transference, dreams will increase, metaphors will crop up with new frequency, and so forth. In short, the supply from the patient's unconscious will be so rich that the doctor will have more than ample material to reveal to his patient. This combined process of pressure away from illness and toward health and analysis of unconscious meanings must proceed at a rate which does not overwhelm the patient and force him into a more serious illness. He needs time to work through the rapidly emerging insights, and time to master his new and more mature way of being and relating to the environment.

This approach is, then, a mixture of intense analysis—it is psychodynamic in every respect—and also a form of behavior therapy. The two complement each other beautifully. I am convinced that pure analysis cannot achieve what this combined approach will bring, and I am equally certain that pure behavior therapy falls equally short in its results. Both types of therapy work to some degree for some patients, but neither works as well alone as the combined approach. I have tested these procedures repeatedly and I am absolutely convinced of this.

Severe behavioral problems, phobias, established sexual patterns—in short, long-standing patterns of living which are maladaptive (pathological)—require a behavioral therapy element in the treatment plan. Occasionally such forms of illness will yield to analysis alone, but they will more often yield to the combined approach of analysis and persistent efforts on the part of therapist and patient to draw upon the willpower of the patient to change his way of being.

If, after a reasonable period of analysis, a symptom (say, frigidity in a woman) does not clear up, the doctor better pay close attention to the way she behaves in bed. He may have to instruct her how to go about it, and as she tries to change her way of behaving with her partner, anxiety or other symptoms will probably appear. Direct messages from her unconscious will appear in abundance in her treatment. I think it is vital for the doctor to decipher these messages and help the patient understand what her unresponsiveness or anxiety is really all about. A high degree of uncooperativeness, repressed hostility, guilt, penis envy, or anxiety associated with closeness may be discovered. This insight needs to be thoroughly worked over at the same time the patient is practicing new and more effective ways of going about the sex act. Given enough persistent effort, good analytic work, encouragement, and advice from the doctor, the chances of success are excellent. Psychoanalysis alone can never do as much for a frigid woman as a combination of (1) treatment, and (2), a good man in bed with her. Instructions from the doctor as to how to cooperate with that man may be necessary. Incidentally, that man in bed should never be the analyst! If the patient is married it should always be the husband. If the husband is troubled by some form of impotence then he too must receive professional help.

The good doctor, the one who really knows what he is doing, will never be content to make the patient's unconscious conflicts conscious and leave the rest up to the patient to change or not to change. He will see to it that the patient changes in a mature direction in the face of this insight. If, for instance, strong infantile erotic ties to the mother are uncovered in a male patient, the doctor will immediately suspect, if he has not already made this discovery, that the patient's relationship with his wife is falling short of what it might be. He will make detailed inquiry into that relationship. The doctor will point out what the patient should stop doing and will advise what he should start doing—if the patient has not already made these observations himself. The doctor will periodically reevaluate the patient's relationship with his wife to see how the patient is progressing, while at the same time analyzing the patient's conflicts. The same principle applies to all other aspects of the patient's life, his children, friends, work, etc. No part of the patient's existence should be immune to careful inspection by the doctor in a treatment endeavor that is geared to bring about maximal changes for the patient. This includes religious beliefs and practices—everything in the patient's life. It is astounding how much

pathology can be uncovered by this approach. If the doctor
works only with what the patient tells him spontaneously,
the treatment will necessarily be limited in its outcome.
Many patients are quite candid about themselves; some,
however, are very guarded and may not even know they
are concealing vital information about themselves from the
doctor.

Bibliography

1. Anshen, R. N., ed. *The Family: Its Function and Destiny*. Vol. 5. (rev. ed.) New York: Harper, 1959.

2. Bartell, Gilbert D. *Group Sex: A Scientist's Eyewitness Report on the American Way of Swinging*. New York: P. H. Wyden, 1971.

3. Bauman, J., "Effects of chronic Marijuana Use on Endocrine Function of Human Females." Read before: Marijuana, Biological Effects and Social Implications. New York: June 28-29 1979.

4. Bieber, I. *Homosexuality–A Psychoanalytic Study*. New York: Basic Books, 1962.

5. Boulding, Elise. Women and Social Violence. *International Social Science Journal* 30 (4): 801-815, 1978.

6. Blum, R. H., et al. *Horatio Alger's Children: The Role of the Family in the Origin and Prevention of Drug Risk*. San Francisco: Jossey-Bass, 1972.

7. Brody, Sylvia. Psychoanalytic Theories of Infant Development and its Disturbances: A Critical Evaluation. *The Psychoanalytic Quarterly* 51 (4): 526-598, 1982.

8. Brownmiller, Susan. *Against Our Will: Men, Women and Rape*; also communication, Conference on Pornography and Male Sexuality, Dec. 2, 1981.

9. Chein. Narcotics Use Among Juveniles. In *Readings in Juvenile Delinquency*, T. Cavan, pp. 237-252. New York: Lippincott, 1964.

10. Chein, et al. The Family of the Addict. In *The Road to H: Narcotics, Delinquency and Social Policy*. I. Chein, pp. 251-275. New York: Basic Books, 1964.

11. Chlor, Harry M. Definitions of Obscenity and the Nature of the Obscene, *Obscenity and Public Morality*. Chicago: University of Chicago Press, 1969.

12. Donnerstein, Edward. Pornography and Violence Against Women: Experimental Studies. *Annals of New York Academy of Sciences* 347:277-288, 1980.

13. Du Maas, Frank M. *Gay Is Not Good*. Nashville: Thomas Nelson, 1979.

14. Gittelson, Natalie. "*Dominus, A Woman Looks at Men's Lives*." New York: Farrar, Straus and Giraux, 1978.

15. Goldberg, S. *The Inevitability of Patriarchy*. New York: Morrow, 1973.

16. Hart, R. H. *Better Grass–The Cruel Truth About Marijuana*. P. O. Box 7542, Shawnee Mission, Kansas: Psychoneurologia Press, 1980.

17. Hartman. Drug-Taking Adolescents. *Psychoanalytic Study of the Child* 24: 384, 1969.

18. Heath, R. G. *Marijuana and the Brain*. American Council on Marijuana, 6193 Executive Boulevard, Rockville, Maryland, 20852.

19. Hendin, Herbert. Homosexuality: The Psychosocial Dimension. *Journal of the American Academy of Psychoanalysis* 6 (1): 479-496, 1978.

20. Jones, H. B. *What the Practicing Physician Should Know About Marijuana*. Private Practice, January, 1980.

21. Kardiner, A. *The Individual and His Society*. New York: Columbia University Press, 1939.

22. Kellman, S. G., Ensminger, M., Turner, J. Family Structure and the Mental Health of Children. *Archives of General Psychiatry*, 34: 1012-1022, September, 1977.

23. Kline, Victor B. *Where Do You Draw the Line? An Exploration into Media Violence, Pornography and Censorship*. Brigham Young University, Press, 1974.

24. Kolodny, R. C., et al. Depression of Plasma Testosterone and Acute Marijuana Administration in *The Pharmocology of Marijuana*, pp. 217-225. Raven Press, 1976.

25. Lasch, Christopher. *Haven in a Heartless World: The Family Besieged*. New York: Basic Books, 1977.

26. Lasch, Christopher. *The Culture of Narcissism: American Life in an Age of Diminishing Expectations*. 1st ed. New York: Norton, 1978, c 1979.

27. Lidz, Theodore. *The Family and Human Adaptation*. New York: International Universities Press, 1963.

28. Lidz, Theodore. The Family: The Source of Human Resources. in *Human Resources and Economic Welfare* by Ivor Berg. New York/ London: Columbia University Press, 1972.

29. Maccoby, E. E., ed. *The Development of Sex Differences*. Stanford: Stanford University Press, 1966.

30. Malamuth, Neal M., Heim, M., Feshbach, S. Sexual Responsiveness of College Students to Rape Depictions: Inhibitory and Disinhibitory Effects. *Journal of Personal and Social Psychology* 38 (3): 399-408.

31. Mann, Peggy. Marijuana Alert III: The Devastation of Personality. *Reader's Digest*, December 1981.

32. Marijuana, Its Health Hazards and Therapeutic Potentials, Council on Scientific Affairs. *Journal of the American Medical Association* 26 (16) October 16, 1981.

33. Millar, Thomas P. The Age of Passion Man. *Canadian Journal of Psychiatry*. 27: 679-682, 1982.

34. Montague, M. F. A., ed. *Culture and the Evolution of Man*. New York: Oxford University Press, 1962.

35. Nahas, G. G. Current Status of Marijuana Research, *Journal of the American Medical Association*. 242:2775, December 21, 1979.

36. *Keep Off the Grass*. New York: Pergamon Press, 1979.

37. *Marijuana–Deceptive Weed*. New York: Raven Press, 1972.

38. Nahas, G. G., Paton, W. D. M. *Marijuana: Biological Effects (Analysis, Metabolism, Cellular Responses, Reproduction, and Brain)*. New York: Pergamon Press, 1979.

39. O'Neil, Neva, O'Neil, George. *Open Marriage, a New Life Style for Couples*. New York: Evans and Company, 1972.

40. Papenoe, Paul. "Fraudulent New 'Morality'". *Medical Aspects of Human Sexuality* 7 (4): 159-167, April, 1973.

41. Powelson, H. *Our Most Dangerous Drug*. Washington: Narcotics Education, Inc., 6830 Laurel St., NW, Washington, D. C., 20012.

42. Riencourt, Omairy de. *Sex and Power in History*. New York: Dell Publishing Company, 1974.

43. Rosenberg, C. M. Young Drug Addicts: Background and Personality. *Journal of Nervous and Mental Disease* 148: 65, 1969.

44. Rosenkrantz, H., Fleishman, R. W. Effect of Cannabis on the Lung. *Marijuana: Biological Effects* (G. G. Nahas and W. D. M. Paton, eds.), pp. 279-299. New York: Pergamon Press, 1979.

45. Russell, George K. *Marijuana Today: A Compilation of Medical Findings for the Layman.* American Council on Marijuana, 6193 Executive Boulevard, Rockville, Maryland, 20852.

46. Savitt, R. A. Psychoanalytic Studies on Addiction: Ego Structure in Narcotic Addiction. *Psychoanalytic Quarterly.* 32 (43), 1963.

47. Seldin, N. E. The Family of the Addict: A Review of the Literature. *International Journal of the Addictions.* 7 (97), 1972.

48. Sexton, P. *The Feminized Male: Classrooms, White Collar and the Decline of Manliness.* New York: Random House, 1969.

49. Smith, C. C., et al. Effect of ^{9} Tetrahydrocannabinol (THC) on female Reproductive Function, *Marijuana: Biological Effects* (G. G. Nahas and W. D. M. Paton, eds.), pp. 449-467. New York: Pergamon Press, 1979.

50. Smith, Malcolm E. *"With Love from Dad."* Book Distributors, Inc., 1978.

51. Socarides, C. W. *The Overt Homosexual.* New York: Grune & Stratton, 1968.

52. *Beyond Sexual Freedom.* New York: Quadrangle, 1975.

53. *Homosexuality.* New York: Jason Aronson, 1978.

54. Sorokin, P. *The American Sex Revolution.* Boston: Sargent Publishers, 1956.

55. Sorokin, P. *Social and Cultural Dynamics.* New York: American Book Co., 1937.

56. Stoller, R. J. Sex and Gender: *The Development of Masculinity and Femininity.* New York: Science House, 1968.

57. Stoller, R. J. Pornography and Perversion. *Perversion: the erotic form of hatred*, pp. 63-92. New York: Pantheon Books (Random House), 1975.

58. Tashkin, D. P., Shapiro, B. J., Lee, Y. E. Subacute Effects of Heavy Marijuana Smoking on Pulmonary Function in Healthy Men. *New England Journal of Medicine.* 294: 125-29, 1976.

59. Tec, N. Family and Differential Involvement with Marijuana: A Study of Suburban Teenagers. *Journal of Marriage and the Family.* 32: 656, 1970.

60. Turner, C., Waller, C. W., et al. *Marijuana, An Annotated Bibliography.* New York: MacMillan Information, Inc., 1976.

61. Unwin, J. D. *Sex and Culture*. London: Oxford University Press, 1934.

62. Voth, H., Orth, M. *Psychotherapy and the Role of the Environment*. New York: Behavioral Publications, 1977.

63. Voth, H. *How To Get Your Child Off Marijuana*. Darien, Conn. Patient Care Publications, 1980.

64. Walk, R. L., Diskind, M. H. Personality dynamics of Mothers and Wives of Drug Addicts. *Crime and Delinquency*. 7: 148, 1961.

65. Wertham, Fredric. Is Exposure to Pornography Harmful to Teenagers? *Journal of the American Medical Association*. 231 (13): 1293, 1975.

66. Wiener, H., Kaplan, E. H. Drug Use in adolescents, Psychodynamic Meaning and Pharmacologic Effect. *Psychoanalytic Study of the Child*. 24: 399, 1969.

Notes

Chapter One

1. U.S. Department of Commerce, Bureau of Census, Current Population Reports, Series p-60, No. 161 (Washington, D.C.: U.S. Government Printing Office, 1990).

2. Ibid., No. 445.

3. Sylvia Brody, M.D. "Psychoanalytic Theories of Infant Development and Its Disturbances: A Critical Evaluation," *Psychoanalytic Quarterly* 51 (October 1982): 526-598.

4. Ibid.

5. R.F. Reinhardt, "The Outstanding Jet Pilot," *American Journal of Psychiatry* 127 (December 1970): 732-736.

6. G.E. Vaillant, "Natural History of Male Psychological Health," *Archives of General Psychiatry* 31 (July 1974): 15-22.

Chapter Five

1. N. Tinbergen, *Social Behavior in Animals* (London: Methuen, 1953).

Chapter Eight

1. See I. Chein, "Narcotics Use Among Juveniles," *Reading in Juvenile Delinquency*, ed. T. Cavan (New York: Lippincott, 1964), 237-252; I. Chein, et al, "The Family of the Addict," *The Road to H: Narcotics, Delinquency and Social Policy*, ed. I. Chein (New York: Basic Books, 1964) 251-275; Dora Hartman, "Drug-Taking Adolescents," *Psychoanalytic Study of the Child* 24 (1969): 384; S.G. Kellman, M. Ensinger, J. Turner, "Family Structure and the Mental Health of Children," *Archives of General Psychiatry* 34 (September 1977): 1012; C.M. Rosenberg, "Young Drug Addicts: Background and Personality," *Journal of Nervous and Mental Disease* 148 (1969): 65; R.A. Savitt, "Psychoanalytic Studies on Addiction: Ego Structure in Narcotic Addiction," *Psychoanalytic Quarterly* 32 (1963): 43; N.E. Seldin, "The Family of the Addict: A Review of the Literature," *International Journal of the Addictions* 7 (1972): 97; N. Tec, "Family and differential Involvement with

223

Marijuana: A Study of Suburban Teen-agers," *Journal of Marriage and the Family* 32 (1970): 656; R.L. Walk, M.H. Diskind, "Personality dynamics of Mothers and Wives of Drug Addicts," *Crime and Delinquency* 7 (1961): 148; H. Wiener, E.H. Kaplan, "Drug Use in Adolescents, Psychodynamic Meaning and Pharmacologic Effect," *Psychoanalytic Study of the Child* 24 (1969): 399.

2. Charles Winick, *The New People: Desexualization in American Life* (Indianapolis: Pegasus, 1968).

3. J. Bowlby, "The Nature of the Child's Tie to His Mother," *International Journal of Psycho-Analysis* 39 (1958): 350-373.

Chapter Nine

1. Theodore Litz, "The Family: The Source of Human Resources," *Human Resources and Economic Welfare*, ed. Ivor Berg (New York/ London: Columbia University Press, 1972); see also R.J. Stoller, *Sex and Gender: The Development of Masculinity and Femininity* (New York: Science House, 1968).

2. Frank M. du Maas, *Gay Is Not Good* (Nashville: Thomas Nelson, 1979); see also E.E. Maccoby, ed., *The Development of Sex Differences* (Stanford: Stanford University Press, 1966).

3. Omairy de Riencourt, *Sex and Power in History* (New York: Dell Publishing Company, 1974).

4. Recognizing its mistake, the army has recently abandoned the co-educational training of recruits.

Chapter Ten

1. I believe this is so because a rise in the prevalence of homosexuality is a function of disturbed family life. When the societies break up, so too have the families. The most classic example is that of ancient Rome. See A. Kardiner, *The Individual and His Society* (New York: Columbia University Press, 1939).

2. The American Psychiatric Association and the American Psychological Association no longer designate homosexuality as a mental disturbance. The *Psychiatric Diagnostic Manual* states homosexuality shall be classed as a psychiatric disturbance only if the individual is bothered by his/her condition. Such reasoning is a laughable, but tragic absurdity. There are many forms of mental disturbance that do not bother the patient; in fact, the patient finds pleasure from his illness! Dr. Charles Socorides had written an article entitled "The Sexual Unreason," reprinted from *Book Forum: in Psychotherapy and Social Structure*, Vol. I, No. 2, 1974, Hudson River Press, N.Y. which

tells the sad story of how this hoax came about. In short, gay lobbying pressure and sleight-of-hand proved to be highly effective.

3. Dr. Charles Socorides, "The Sexual Unreason," reprinted from *Book Forum: in Psychotherapy and Social Structure* 1 (New York: Hudson River Press, 1974).

4. Herbert Hendin, "Homosexuality: the Psychosocial Dimension," *Journal of the American Academy Psychoanalysis* 6 (1978): 479-496. In this article the author reports that the family patterns of homosexuals who were not classed as psychiatric patients are the same as those who are. Homosexuals in their claim that nothing is wrong with them point to the fact that most studies of homosexuals were done on psychiatric patients who were also homosexual.

5. I. Bieber, *Homosexuality–A Psychoanalytic Study* (New York: Basic Books, 1962). Bieber's work is a classic. His findings are entirely consistent with the in-depth data psychoanalyists have reported.

6. Charles Socorides, *The Overt Homosexual* (New York: Grune and Stratton, 1968); Socorides, *Beyond Sexual Freedom* (New York: Quadrangle, 1975); Frank M. du Maas, *Gay Is Not Good* (Nashville: Thomas Nelson, 1979).

Chapter Eleven

1. Sylvia Brody, M.D., "Psychoanalytic Theories of Infant Development and Its Disturbances: A Critical Evaluation," *The Psychoanalytic Quarterly* 51 (October 1982): 526-598; Neal M. Malamuth, M. Heim, S. Feshbach, "Sexual Responsiveness of College Students to Rape Depictions: Inhibitory and Disinhibitory Effects," *Journal of Personal and Social Psychology* 38 (n.d.): 399-408.

Selected Readings

1. Anshen, R. N., ed. *The Family: Its Function and Destiny.* Vol. 5. rev. ed. New York: Harper, 1959.

2. Anthony, E. J., and T. Benedek, eds. *Parenthood–Its Psychology and Psychopathology.* Boston: Little, Brown, 1970.

3. Ardrey, R. *African Genesis.* New York: Atheneum, 1961.

4. *The Territorial Imperative.* New York: Atheneum, 1966.

5. Bartell, Gilbert D. *Group Sex: A Scientist's Eyewitness Report on the American Way of Swinging.* New York: P. H. Wyden, 1971.

6. Bauman, J., "Effects of Chronic Marijuana Use on Endocrine Function of Human Females" Read before: *Marijuana, Biological Effects and Social Implications.* New York, June 28-29, 1979.

7. Beach, F. A., ed. *Sex and Behavior.* New York: Wiley, 1965.

8. Benedek, T. *Psychosexual Functions of Women.* New York: Ronald Press, 1952.

9. Benson, L. *Fatherhood.* New York: Random House, 1968.

10. Bettelheim, B. *The Children of the Dream.* New York: Macmillan, 1969.

11. "Young Radicals Emotionally Ill." *Kansas City Star,* 22 September 1970.

12. Bieber, I. et al. *Homosexuality.* New York: Basic Books, 1962.

13. Blum, R. H., et al. *Horatio Alger's Children: The Role of the Family in the Origin and Prevention of Drug Risk.* San Francisco: Jossey-Bass, 1972.

14. Bonaparte, M. *Female Sexuality.* New York: International Universities Press, 1953.

15. Boulding, Elise. "Women and Social Violence." *International Social Science Journal* 30 (1978): 801-815.

16. Bowlby, J. "The Nature of the Child's Tie to his Mother." *International Journal of Psycho-Analysis* 39 (1958): 350-373.

17. *Attachment and Loss.* Vol. 1. New York: Basic Books, 1969.

18. *Separation.* Vol. 2. New York: Basic Books, 1973.

19. Bratter, T. E. "Treating Alienated, Unmotivated, Drug Abusing Adolescents." *American Journal of Psychotherapy* 27 (1973): 585-598.

20. Brenner, C. *An Elementary Textbook of Psychoanalysis.* New York: International Universities Press, 1955.

21. Brenton, M. *The American Male.* New York: Coward-McCann, 1966.

22. Brody, Sylvia. *Patterns of Mothering; Maternal Influence During Infancy.* New York: International Universities Press, 1956.

23. "Psychoanalytic Theories of Infant Development and its Disturbances: A Critical Evaluation." *The Psychoanalytic Quarterly* 51 (1982): 526-598.

24. Brownmiller, Susan. *Against Our Will: Men, Women and Rape*; also communication, "Conference on Pornography and Male Sexuality," 2 December 1981.

25. Chein. "Narcotics Use Among Juveniles." In *Readings in Juvenile Delinquency*, edited by T. Cavan, 237-252. New York: Lippincott, 1964.

26. Chein, et al. "The Family of the Addict." In *The Road to H: Narcotics, Delinquency and Social Policy.* edited by I. Chein, 251-275. New York: Basic Books, 1964.

27. Chessick, R. D. *How Psychotherapy Heals.* New York: Science House, 1969.

28. *Why Psychotherapists Fail.* New York: Science House, 1971.

29. Chlor, Harry M. "Definitions of Obscenity and the Nature of the Obscene." *Obscenity and Public Morality.* Chicago: University of Chicago Press, 1969.

30. de Riencourt, Omairy. *Sex and Power in History.* New York: Dell Publishing Company, 1974.

31. Deutsch, H. *The Psychology of Women.* 2 vols. New York: Grune and Stratton, 1944-1945.

32. *Confrontations with Myself.* New York: Norton, 1973.

33. DeVore, I. *Primate Behavior.* New York: Holt, Rinehart and Winston, 1965.

34. Donnerstein, Edward. "Pornography and Violence Against Women: Experimental Studies." *Annals of New York Academy of Sciences* 347 (1980): 277-288.

35. Du Maas, Frank M. *Gay Is Not Good.* Nashville: Thomas Nelson, 1979.

36. Engel, G. *Psychological Development in Health and Disease*. Philadelphia: Saunders, 1962.

37. Erikson, E. H. *Childhood and Society*. New York: Norton, 1964.

38. Escalona, S. K. *The Roots of Individuality; Normal Patterns of Development in Infancy*. Chicago: Aldine, 1968.

39. Farber, S. M., and R.H.L. Wilson, eds. *Man and Civilization: The Potential of Women*. New York: McGraw-Hill, 1963.

40. Fenichel, O. *The Psychoanalytic Theory of Neurosis*. New York: Norton, 1945.

41. Fisher, S. *The Female Orgasm: Psychology, Physiology, Fantasy*. New York: Basic Books, 1973.

42. Ford, D. H., and H. B. Urban. *Systems of Psychotherapy*. New York: Wiley, 1963.

43. Freedman, A. M., and Kaplan, H. I., eds. *Comprehensive Textbook of Psychiatry*. Baltimore: Williams & Wilkins, 1967.

44. Freud, S. *The Ego and the Mechanisms of Defense*. New York: International Universities Press, 1946.

45. *The Problem of Anxiety*. New York: Norton, 1936.

46. *An Outline of Psychoanalysis*. New York: Norton, 1949.

47. *The Interpretation of Dreams*. New York: Basic Books, 1955.

48. *Collected Papers*. 5 vols. New York: Basic Books, 1957.

49. *The Complete Introductory Lectures on Psychoanalysis*. New York: Norton, 1966.

50. Gadpaille, W. J. "Research into the Physiology of Maleness and Femaleness." *Archives of General Psychiatry* 26 (1972): 193-206.

51. Gittelson, Natalie. *Dominus, A Woman Looks at Men's Lives*. New York: Farrar, Straus and Giraux, 1978.

52. Glover, E. *The Technique of Psychoanalysis*. New York: International Universities Press, 1955.

53. Goldberg, S. *The Inevitability of Patriarchy*. New York: Morrow, 1973.

54. Green, R., et al. "Treatment of Boyhood Transsexualism." *Archives of General Psychiatry* 26 (1972): 213-217.

55. Greenson, R. R. *The Technique and Practice of Psychoanalysis*. New York: International Universities Press, 1967.

56. Group for the Advancement of Psychiatry. *The Joys and Sorrows of Parenthood*. Report no. 84, vol. 8. New York: Group for the Advancement of Psychiatry, 1973.

57. Hall, C. S., and G. Lindzey. *Theories of Personality.* 2d ed. New York: Wiley, 1973.

58. Handel, G. *The Psychosocial Interior of the Family.* Chicago: Aldine, 1967.

59. Harlow, H. F., and M. K. Harlow. "Social Deprivation in Monkeys." *Scientific American* 207 (1962): 136-146.

60. "The Effect of Rearing Conditions on Behavior." In *Sex Research: New Developments,* edited by J. Money, 161-175. New York: Holt, Rinehart and Winston, 1965.

61. Harris, G. W. "Sex Hormones, Brain Development, and Brain Function." *Endocrinology* 175 (1964): 627-648.

62. Hart, R. H. *Better Grass–The Cruel Truth About Marijuana* Shawnee Mission, Kansas: Psychoneurologia Press, 1980.

63. Hartman, Dora. "Drug-Taking Adolescents." *Psychoanalytic Study of the Child* 24 (1969): 384.

64. Heath, R. G. *Marijuana and the Brain.* Rockville, Maryland: American Council on Marijuana, 1981.

65. Jones, H. B., *What the Practicing Physician Should Know About Marijuana.* Private Practice, January, 1980.

66. Josselyn, I. M. *Psychosocial Development of Children.* New York: Family Service Assn. of America, 1948.

67. Kardiner, A. *The Individual and His Society.* New York: Columbia University Press, 1939.

68. Katchadourian, H. A. and D. T. Lunde. *Fundamentals of Human Sexuality.* 2d ed. New York: Holt, Rinehart and Winston, 1975.

69. Kellman, S. G., M. Ensminger, J. Turner. "Family Structure and the Mental Health of Children." *Archives of General Psychiatry* 34 (1977): 1012-1022.

70. Klein, M. *The Psycho-Analysis of Children.* London: Hogarth, 1963.

71. Kline, Victor B. *Where Do You Draw the Line? An Exploration into Media Violence, Pornography and Censorship.* Salt Lake City: Brigham Young University Press, 1974.

72. Kolodny, R. C., et al. "Depression of Plasma Testosterone and Acute Marijuana Administration." In *The Pharmocology of Marijuana,* 217-225. Lancaster, Ca.: Raven Press, 1976.

73. Lasch, Christopher. *Haven in a Heartless World: The Family Besieged.* New York: Basic Books, 1977.

74. *The Culture of Narcissism: American Life in an Age of Diminishing Expectations.* 1st ed. New York: Norton, 1978, c 1979.

75. LeMasters, E. E. *Parents in Modern America*. Homewood, Ill.: Dorsey Press, 1970.

76. Lesse, S. "Jane Doe and Our Future Society—Searching for an Image." *American Journal of Psychotherapy* 17 (1973): 333-337, .

77. Levy, D. M. *Maternal Overprotection*. New York: Columbia University Press, 1943.

78. Lidz, T. *The Family and Human Adaptation*. New York: International Universities Press, 1963.

79. "The Family: The Source of Human Resources." In *Human Resources and Economic Welfare* edited by Ivor Berg. New York/London: Columbia University Press, 1972.

80. Lorenz, K. *On Aggression*. New York: Harcourt, Brace, 1966.

81. *Studies in Animal and Human Behavior*. 2 vols. Cambridge, Mass.: Harvard University Press, 1970-1971.

82. Maccoby, E. E., ed. *The Development of Sex Differences*. Stanford: Stanford University Press, 1966.

83. Malamuth, Neal M., M. Heim, S. Feshbach. "Sexual Responsiveness of College Students to Rape Depictions: Inhibitory and Disinhibitory Effects." *Journal of Personal and Social Psychology* 38 (1980): 399-408.

84. Mann, Peggy. "Marijuana Alert III: The Devastation of Personality." *Reader's Digest*, December 1981.

85. "Marijuana, Its Health Hazards and Therapeutic Potentials, Council on Scientific Affairs."*Journal of the American Medical Association* 26 (16 October 1981).

86. Marmor, J., ed. *Sexual Inversion*. New York: Basic Books, 1965.

87. Masters, W. H., and V. E. Johnson *Human Sexual Inadequacy*. Boston: Little, Brown, 1970.

88. Menninger, K. *The Theory of Psychoanalytic Technique*. New York: Basic Books, 1958.

89. Menninger, K., et al. *The Vital Balance*. New York: Viking Press, 1963.

90. Millar, Thomas P. "The Age of Passion Man." *Canadian Journal of Psychiatry* 27(1982): 679-682.

91. Miller, D. R., and G. E. Swanson. *The Changing American Parent*. New York: Wiley, 1958.

92. Montagu, M. F. A., ed. *Culture and the Evolution of Man*. New York: Oxford University Press, 1962.

93. Nahas, G. G. "Current Status of Marijuana Research." *Journal of the American Medical Association* 242 (21 December 1979): 2775.

94. *Keep Off the Grass.* New York: Pergamon Press, 1979.

95. *Marijuana–Deceptive Weed.* New York: Raven Press, 1972.

96. Nahas, G. G., W. D. M. Paton. *Marijuana: Biological Effects (Analysis, Metabolism, Cellular Responses, Reproduction, and Brain).* New York: Pergamon Press, 1979.

97. O'Neil, Neva, George O'Neil. *Open Marriage, a New Life Style for Couples.* New York: Evans and Company, 1972.

98. Parsons, T., and R. Bales, eds. *Family, Socialization and Interaction Process.* Glencoe, Ill.: Free Press, 1955.

99. Popenoe, P. "The Fraudulent New 'Morality.'" *Medical Aspects of Human Sexuality* 7 (April 1973): 159-167.

100. Powelson, H. *Our Most Dangerous Drug.* Washington: Narcotics Education, Inc., n.d.

101. Reinhardt, R. F. "The Outstanding Jet Pilot." *American Journal of Psychiatry* 127(December 1970): 732-736.

102. Rheingold, H. L., ed. *Maternal Behavior in Mammals.* New York: Wiley, 1963.

103. Rheingold, J. C. *The Fear of Being a Woman.* New York: Grune and Stratton, 1964.

104. Rosenberg, C. M. "Young Drug Addicts: Background and Personality." *Journal of Nervous and Mental Disease* 148 (1969): 65.

105. Rosenkrantz, H., R. W. Fleishman. "Effect of Cannabis on the Lung." In *Marijuana: Biological Effects,* edited by G. G. Nahas and W. D. M. Paton, 279-299. New York: Pergamon Press, 1979.

106. Russell, George K. *Marijuana Today: A Compilation of Medical Findings for the Layman.* Rockville, Maryland: American Council on Marijuana, 1983.

107. Salk, L. "When to Spoil Your Baby." *Newsweek,* 13 March 1972, 53.

108. Savitt, R. A. "Psychoanalytic Studies on Addiction: Ego Structure in Narcotic Addiction." *Psychoanalytic Quarterly* 32 (1963): 43.

109. Seldin, N. E. The Family of the Addict: A Review of the Literature. *International Journal of the Addictions* 7 (1972): 97.

110. Sexton, P. *The Feminized Male: Classrooms, White Collar and the Decline of Manliness.* New York: Random House, 1969.

111. Smith, C. C., et al. "Effect of Λ^9-Tetrahydrocannabinol (THC) on Female Reproductive Function." In *Marijuana: Biological Effects* edited by G. G. Nahas and W. D. M. Paton, 449-467. New York: Pergamon Press, 1979.

112. Smith, Malcolm E. *With Love from Dad.* n.p.: Book Distributors, Inc., 1978.

113. Socarades, C. W. *The Overt Homosexual.* New York: Grune and Stratton, 1968.

114. *Beyond Sexual Freedom.* New York: Quadrangle, 1975.

115. *Beyond Sexual Freedom.* New York: Quadrangle, 1975.

116. *Homosexuality.* New York: Jason Aronson, 1978.

117. Sorokin, P. *The American Sex Revolution.* Boston: Sargent Publishers, 1956.

118. *Social and Cultural Dynamics.* New York: American Book Co., 1937.

119. Spiegel, J., and N. Bell. "The Family of the Psychiatric Patient." In *American Handbook of Psychiatry* edited by S. Arieti. New York: Basic Books, 1959.

120. Spitz, R. A. "Hospitalism: An Inquiry into the Genesis of Psychiatric Conditions in Early Childhood." *Psychoanalytic Study of the Child* 1(1945): 53-74.

121. *The First Year of Life.* New York: International Universities Press, 1965.

122. Steppocher, R. C., and J. S. Mausner. "Suicide in Male and Female Physicians." *Journal of the American Medical Association* 228 (15 April 1974): 323-328.

123. Stoller, R. J. *Sex and Gender: The Development of Masculinity and Femininity.* New York: Science House, 1968.

124. "Pornography and Perversion." In *Perversion: the Erotic Form of Hatred*, 63-92. New York: Pantheon Books (Random House), 1975.

125. "The 'Bedrock' of Masculinity and Femininity: Bisexuality." *Archives of General Psychiatry* 26 (1972): 207-212.

126. Tashkin, D. P., B. J. Shapiro, Y. E. Lee. "Subacute Effects of Heavy Marijuana Smoking on Pulmonary Function in Healthy Men." *New England Journal of Medicine* 294 (1976): 125-129.

127. Tec, N. "Family and Differential Involvement with Marijuana: A Study of Suburban Teenagers." *Journal of Marriage and the Family* 32 (1970): 656.

128. Thompson, C. M. "Interpersonal Psychoanalysis." In *Selected Papers of Clara M. Thompson,* edited by M. R. Green. New York: Basic Books, 1964.

129. Tinbergen, N. *The Study of Instinct.* Oxford, England.: Clarendon Press, 1951.

130. *Social Behavior in Animals.* London: Methuen, 1953.

131. Turner, C., C. W. Waller, et al. *Marijuana, An Annotated Bibliography*. New York: MacMillan Information, Inc., 1976.

132. Unwin, J. D. *Sex and Culture*. London: Oxford University Press, 1934.

133. Vaillant, G. E. "Natural History of Male Psychological Health." *Archives of General Psychiatry* 31(July 1974): 15-22.

134. Voth, H. M. *How To Get Your Child Off Marijuana*. Darien, Conn.: Patient Care Publications, 1980.

135. "Some Effects of Freud's Personality on Psychoanalytic Theory and Technique." *International Journal of Psychiatry* 10 (1972): 48-69.

136. "Responsibility in the Practice of Psychoanalysis and Psychotherapy. *American Journal of Psychotherapy* 26 (1972): 69-83.

137. Voth, H. M., and M. H. Orth. *Psychotherapy and the Role of the Environment*. New York: Behavioral Publications, 1973.

138. *Psychotherapy and the Role of the Environment*. New York: Behavioral Publications, 1977.

139. Waelder, R. *Basic Theory of Psychoanalysis*. New York: International Universities Press, 1960.

140. Wainwright, W. H. "Fatherhood as a Precipitant of Mental Illness." *American Journal of Psychiatry* 123 (1966): 40-44.

141. Walk, R. L., M. H. Diskind. "Personality Dynamics of Mothers and Wives of Drug Addicts." *Crime and Delinquency* 7(1961): 148.

142. Washburn, S. L., ed. *Social Life of Early Man*. Chicago: Aldine, 1961.

143. Wertham, Fredric. "Is Exposure to Pornography Harmful to Teen-agers?" *Journal of the American Medical Association* 231 (1975): 1293 .

144. Wiener, H., E. H. Kaplan. "Drug Use in Adolescents, Psychodynamic Meaning and Pharmacologic Effect." *Psychoanalytic Study of the Child* 24 (1969): 399.

145. Winick, C. E. *The New People: Desexualization in American Life*. Indianapolis: Pegasus, 1968.

146. Winick, C. E. "Six and Society: Unisex in America." *Medical Opinion & Review* 6 (1970): 62-65.

147. Yates, A. J. *Behavior Therapy*. New York: Wiley, 1970.

148. Wade, N. "Bottle-Feeding: Adverse Effects of a Western Technology" *Science* 184 (5 April 1974): 45-48.

MORE GOOD BOOKS FROM
HUNTINGTON HOUSE PUBLISHERS

RECENT RELEASES

Gays & Guns
The Case Against Homosexuals in the Military
by John Eidsmoe

The homosexual revolution seeks to overthrow the Laws of Nature. A Lieutenant Colonel in the United States Air Force Reserve, Dr. John Eidsmoe eloquently contends that admitting gays into the military would weaken the combat effectiveness of our armed forces. This cataclysmic step would also legitimize homosexuality, a lifestyle that most Americans know is wrong.

While echoing Cicero's assertion that "a sense of what is right is common to all mankind," Eidsmoe rationally defends his belief. There are laws that govern the universe, he reminds us. Laws that compel the earth to rotate on its axis, laws that govern the economy; and so there is also a moral law that governs man's nature. The violation of this moral law is physically, emotionally and spiritually destructive. It is destructive to both the individual and to the community of which he is a member.

ISBN Trade Paper 1-56384-043-X $7.99
ISBN Hardcover 1-56384-046-4 $14.99

Trojan Horse—
How the New Age Movement Infiltrates the Church
by Samantha Smith &
Brenda Scott

New Age/Occult concepts and techniques are being introduced into all major denominations. The revolution is subtle, cumulative, and deadly. Through what door has this heresy entered the church? Authors Samantha Smith and Brenda Scott attempt to demonstrate that Madeleine L'Engle has been and continues to be a major New Age source of entry into the church. Because of her radical departure from traditional Christian theology, Madeleine L'Engle's writings have sparked a wave of controversy across the nation. She has been published and promoted by numerous magazines, including *Today's Christian Woman, Christianity Today* and others. The deception, unfortunately, has been so successful that otherwise discerning congregations and pastors have fallen into the snare that has been laid.

Sadly, many Christians are embracing the demonic doctrines of the New Age movement. Well hidden under "Christian" labels, occult practices, such as Zen meditation, altered states, divinations, out of body experiences, "discovering the Divine truth within" and others have defiled many. This book explores the depths of infiltration and discusses ways to combat it.

ISBN 1-56384-040-5 $9.99

A Jewish Conservative Looks at Pagan America
by Don Feder

With eloquence and insight that rival contemporary commentators and essayists of antiquity, Don Feder's pen finds his targets in the enemies of God, family, and American tradition and morality. Deftly ... delightfully ... the master allegorist and Titian with a typewriter brings clarity to the most complex sociological issues and invokes giggles and wry smiles from both followers and foes. Feder is Jewish to the core, and he finds in his Judaism no inconsistency with an American Judeo-Christian ethic. Questions of morality plague school administrators, district court judges, senators, congressmen, parents, and employers; they are wrestling for answers in a "changing world." Feder challenges this generation and directs inquirers to the original books of wisdom: the Torah and the Bible.

ISBN 1-56384-036-7 Trade Paper $9.99
ISBN 1-56384-037-5 Hardcover $19.99

Don't Touch That Dial: The Impact of the Media on Children and the Family
by Barbara Hattemer & Robert Showers

Men and women without any stake in the outcome of the war between the pornographers and our families have come to the qualified, professional agreement that media does have an effect on our children—an effect that is devastatingly significant. Highly respected researchers, psychologists, and sociologists join a bevy of pediatricians, district attorneys, parents, teachers, pastors, and community leaders—who have diligently remained true to the fight against pornographic media—in their latest comprehensive critique of the modern media establishment (i.e., film, television, print, art, curriculum).

ISBN 1-56384-032-4 Trade Paper $9.99
ISBN 1-56384-035-9 Hardcover $19.99

Political Correctness: The Cloning of the American Mind
by David Thibodaux, Ph.D.

The author, a professor of literature at the University of Southwestern Louisiana, confronts head on the movement that is now being called Political Correctness. Political correctness, says Thibodaux, "is an umbrella under which advocates of civil rights, gay and lesbian rights, feminism, and environmental causes have gathered." To incur the wrath of these groups, one only has to disagree with them on political, moral, or social issues. To express traditionally Western concepts in universities today can result in not only ostracism, but even suspension. (According to a recent "McNeil-Lehrer News Hour" report, one student was suspended for discussing the reality of the moral law with an avowed homosexual. He was reinstated only after he apologized.)

ISBN 1-56384-026-X Trade Paper $9.99

Subtle Serpent:
New Age in the Classroom
by Darylann Whitemarsh &
Bill Reisman

There is a new morality being taught to our children in public schools. Without the consent or even awareness of parents—educators and social engineers are aggressively introducing new moral codes to our children. In most instances, these new moral codes contradict traditional values. Darylann Whitemarsh (a 1989 Teacher of the Year recipient) and Bill Reisman (educator and expert on the occult) combine their knowledge to expose the deliberate madness occurring in our public schools.

ISBN 1-56384-016-2 $9.99

When the Wicked Seize a City
by Chuck & Donna McIlhenny with Frank York

A highly publicized lawsuit . . . a house fire-bombed in the night . . . the shatter of windows smashed by politically (and wickedly) motivated vandals cuts into the night. . . . All this because Chuck McIlhenny voiced God's condemnation of a behavior and life-style and protested the destruction of society that results from its practice. That behavior is homosexuality, and that life-style is the gay culture. This book explores: the rise of gay power and what it will mean if Christians do not organize and prepare for the battle.

ISBN 1-56384-024-3 $9.99

Loyal Opposition:
A Christian Response to the Clinton Agenda
by John Edismoe

The night before the November 1992 elections, a well-known evangelist claims to have had a dream. In this dream, he says, God told him that Bill Clinton would be elected President, and Christians should support his Presidency. **What are we to make of this?** Does it follow that, because God **allowed** Clinton to be President; therefore, God **wants** Clinton to be president? Does God **want** everything that God **allows**? Is it possible for an event to occur even though that event displeases God? **How do we stand firm in our opposition to the administration's proposals when those proposals contradict Biblical values?** And how do we organize and work effectively for constructive action to restore our nation to basic values?

ISBN 1-56384-044-8 $7.99

Deadly Deception

by Jim Shaw & Tom McKenney

For the first time the 33 degree ritual is made public! Learn of the "secrets" and "deceptions" that are practiced daily around the world. Find out why Freemasonry teaches that it is the true religion, that all other religions are only corrupted and perverted forms of Freemasonry. If you know anyone in the Masonic movement, you must read this book.

ISBN 0-910311-54-4 $7.99

Exposing the AIDS Scandal

by Dr. Paul Cameron

Where do you turn when those who control the flow of information in this country withhold the truth? Why is the national media hiding facts from the public? Can AIDS be spread in ways we're not being told? Finally, a book that gives you a total account for the AIDS epidemic, and what steps can be taken to protect yourself. What you don't know can kill you!

ISBN 0-910311-52-8 $7.99

Hidden Dangers of the Rainbow

by Constance Cumbey

The first book to uncover and expose the New Age movement, this national #1 best-seller paved the way for all other books on the subject. It has become a giant in its category. This book provides the vivid exposé of the New Age movement, which the author contends is dedicated to wiping out Christianity and establishing a one world order. This movement, a vast network of occult and pagan organizations, meets the tests of prophecy concerning the Antichrist.

ISBN 0-910311-03-X $8.99

Kinsey, Sex and Fraud:
The Indoctrination of a People
by Dr. Judith A. Reisman and Edward Eichel

Kinsey, Sex and Fraud describes the research of Alfred Kinsey which shaped Western society's beliefs and understanding of the nature of human sexuality. His unchallenged conclusions are taught at every level of education—elementary, high school and college—and quoted in textbooks as undisputed truth.

The authors clearly demonstrate that Kinsey's research involved illegal experimentations on several hundred children. The survey was carried out on a non-representative group of Americans, including disproportionately large numbers of sex offenders, prostitutes, prison inmates and exhibitionists.

ISBN 0-910311-20-X Hardcover $19.99

Journey into Darkness: Nowhere to Land
by Stephen L. Arrington

This story begins on Hawaii's glistening sands and ends in the mysterious deep of the Great White Shark. In between, he found himself trapped in the drug smuggling trade—unwittingly becoming the "Fall Guy" in the highly publicized John Z. DeLorean drug case. Naval career shattered, his youthful innocence tested, and friends and family put to the test of loyalty, Arrington locked on one truth during his savage stay in prison and endeavors to share that critical truth now. Focusing on a single important message to young people—to stay away from drugs—the author recounts his horrifying prison experience and allows the reader to take a peek at the source of hope and courage that helped him survive.

ISBN 1-56384-003-3 $9.99

"Soft Porn" Plays Hardball
by Dr. Judith A. Reisman

With amazing clarity, the author demonstrates that pornography imposes on society a view of women and children that encourages violence and sexual abuse. As crimes against women and children increase to alarming proportions, it's of paramount importance that we recognize the cause of this violence. Pornography should be held accountable for the havoc it has wreaked in our homes and our country.

ISBN 0-910311-65-X Trade Paper $8.99
ISBN 0-910311-92-7 Hardcover $16.95

Order These Huntington House Books !

_____	America Betrayed—Marlin Maddoux	$6.99 _____
_____	Angel Vision (A Novel)—Jim Carroll with Jay Gaines	5.99 _____
_____	Battle Plan: Equipping the Church for the 90s—Chris Stanton	7.99 _____
_____	Blessings of Liberty—Charles C. Heath	8.99 _____
_____	Crystalline Connection (A Novel)—Bob Maddux	8.99 _____
_____	Deadly Deception: Freemasonry—Tom McKenney	7.99 _____
_____	The Delicate Balance—John Zajac	8.99 _____
_____	Dinosaurs and the Bible—Dave Unfred	12.99 _____
_____	*Don't Touch That Dial—Barbara Hattemer & Robert Showers	9.99/19.99 _____
_____	En Route to Global Occupation—Gary Kah	9.99 _____
_____	Exposing the AIDS Scandal—Dr. Paul Cameron	7.99 _____
_____	Face the Wind—Gloria Delaney	9.99 _____
_____	*False Security—Jerry Parks	9.99 _____
_____	From Rock to Rock—Eric Barger	8.99 _____
_____	*Gays & Guns—John Eidsmoe	7.99 _____
_____	Hidden Dangers of the Rainbow—Constance Cumbey	8.99 _____
_____	*Hitler and the New Age—Bob Rosio	9.99 _____
_____	Inside the New Age Nightmare—Randall Baer	8.99 _____
_____	*A Jewish Conservative Looks at Pagan America—Don Feder	9.99/19.99 _____
_____	*Journey Into Darkness—Stephen Arrington	9.99 _____
_____	Kinsey, Sex and Fraud—Dr. Judith A. Reisman & Edward Eichel (Hard cover)	19.99 _____
_____	Last Days Collection—Last Days Ministries	8.95 _____
_____	Legend of the Holy Lance (A Novel)—William T. Still	8.99/16.99 _____
_____	New World Order—William T. Still	8.99 _____
_____	*One Year to a College Degree—Lynette Long & Eileen Hershberger	9.99 _____
_____	*Political Correctness—David Thibodaux	9.99 _____
_____	Psychic Phenomena Unveiled—John Anderson	8.99 _____
_____	* Real Men—Dr. Harold Voth	9.99 _____
_____	"Soft Porn" Plays Hardball—Dr. Judith A. Reisman	8.99/16.95 _____
_____	*Subtle Serpent—Darylann Whitemarsh & Bill Reisman	9.99 _____
_____	Teens and Devil-Worship—Charles G.B. Evans	8.99 _____
_____	To Grow By Storybook Readers—Janet Friend	44.95 per set _____
_____	Touching the Face of God—Bob Russell (Paper/Hardcover)	8.99/18.99 _____
_____	Trojan Horse—Brenda Scott & Samantha Smith	9.99 _____
_____	Twisted Cross—Joseph Carr	9.99 _____
_____	*When the Wicked Seize a City—Chuck & Donna McIlhenny with Frank York	9.99 _____
_____	Who Will Rule the Future?—Paul McGuire	8.99 _____
_____	*You Hit Like a Girl—Elsa Houtz & William J. Ferkile	9.99 _____

* New Title   Shipping and Handling _____

                        Total _____

AVAILABLE AT BOOKSTORES EVERYWHERE or order direct from:
Huntington House Publishers • P.O. Box 53788 • Lafayette, LA 70505
Send check/money order. For faster service use VISA/MASTERCARD
call toll-free 1-800-749-4009.

Add: Freight and handling, $3.50 for the first book ordered, and $.50 for each additional book up to 5 books.

Enclosed is $_____ including postage.
VISA/MASTERCARD#_____ Exp. Date_____
Name_____ Phone: (   )_____
Address_____
City, State, Zip_____